Balanced

A COMPLEX EQUATION

Body

&

Mind

C.J. BYRNE

P & P PUBLICATIONS

First published in 2020 by

P & P Publications

Dublin

Ireland

balancedbodyandmind1@gmail.com

Amazon paperback edition	ISBN: 978 1 78846 174 0
Paperback	ISBN: 978 1 78846 171 9
eBook – mobi format	ISBN: 978 1 78846 172 6
eBook – ePub format	ISBN: 978 1 78846 173 3

A CIP catalogue record for this book is
available from the British Library

Produced by Kazoo Independent Publishing Services
222 Beech Park, Lucan, Co. Dublin
www.kazoopublishing.com

Kazoo Independent Publishing Services is not the publisher of this work. All rights and responsibilities pertaining to this work remain with P & P Publications.

Cover design by Andrew Brown

Printed in the EU

Bala

A COMPLE

Bo

Mind

I dedicate this book to all those who endure struggles with different areas of their lives that negatively impact their happiness and wellbeing. I wish them every success in overcoming these challenges and becoming the person they want to be.

THANK YOU

I would like to convey a huge thank you to my husband and two sons for all their help and support during the writing of this book.

Contents

Introduction		vii
One	*Obesity*	11
Two	*Where to Start*	24
Three	*Belief System*	28
Four	*Happiness*	37
Five	*Emotions*	45
Six	*Fear*	51
Seven	*Hormones*	55
Eight	*Sleep*	60
Nine	*Stress*	63
Ten	*Values*	70
Eleven	*Behaviours*	74
Twelve	*Habits*	84
Thirteen	*Actions*	88
Fourteen	*Goals*	100
Fifteen	*Exercise*	107
Sixteen	*Nutrition*	124
Seventeen	*Vitamins*	148
Eighteen	*Minerals*	152
Nineteen	*Food Diary*	156
Twenty	*Food Labelling*	161
Twenty-One	*Healthy Happy Life*	167
Courses and Qualifications		173
Index		174

Introduction

Over the past ten years or so, I have attended various courses. Originally, this was to help me gain knowledge on how to enhance and improve the quality of my own life. I completed courses in life and business coaching, exercise and fitness instruction and personal training, health and fitness and personal nutrition. Once I had completed them, I realised there was so much information I had acquired that could help others.

First of all, I thought of setting up a class. As I was trying to put the information together, I changed my mind and decided to develop it into a book. I am neither a writer nor a counsellor, nor indeed, a doctor. However, I genuinely believe that what I have learned over the years could be beneficial information for the reader about health and wellbeing. Even though this book is centred more on losing weight, I also feel it could help with other areas in your life that you may struggle with or want to explore.

There is such a struggle with obesity at the moment. In my opinion, it's not solely because people are sitting around all day doing nothing and overeating. There are numerous reasons and maybe that's why many of us find it difficult to lose weight and keep it off. Many just concentrate on diet and exercise, but other areas in your life come into play, such as stress and sleep.

There's also the concern about what other people think of you. Maybe you think you have to be perfect or struggle to get out of your comfort zone. We have this idea that we can't let our guard down. We don't want people to know we can't cope; we feel we need to make them think everything is perfect. It's okay to say you need some support. It's okay to say you need some help. It's okay to say you are struggling. It doesn't mean you're weak. It means you are strong and not afraid to let people know that you are not perfect. After all, what is perfect? I've never seen it. I see many do their best and to me, that's good enough. If you feel you are not doing what you need to do to achieve a life that you want, at the very least ask yourself why:

- » Why am I afraid to do certain things?
- » Why am I concerned about what other people think?
- » Why am I afraid to let myself go?
- » Why won't I get out of my comfort zone?

I know for sure that if you get out of your comfort zone and accomplish something, you feel amazing. Bottom line, it's about you taking responsibility for your life, your health and your happiness. No matter what you do, or where you go, what help you get, it's you that will be the primary source of your success.

So, if you think this book is going to "fix" you, it's not! It is you that's going to do that by addressing whatever you need to address to get what you want. It has nothing to do with anyone else – no book or class can do it for you. They are there to help you and they certainly can. However, ultimately, it's down to you and your ability to reach your goals with whatever knowledge and help you pick up along the way. I'm not saying that it's easy to take a good, hard look at yourself and try to change a lifetime of beliefs, behaviours and habits. But for you to achieve your goals, they need to be challenged. To change something, you need to do something different. If you don't change your behaviours then you will stay the way you are.

I look at myself. I completed this book but was afraid to publish it. I am overweight and felt people would think "She's not doing what she says in the book, so obviously it doesn't help," but that's the whole point. This book is not about me and what I do or don't do, or what anybody else does or doesn't do. It's not about "That worked for him or her, so I'll do that." It's about finding what works for *you* and doing that. It's about looking at areas in your life and challenging them.

I have lost weight in the past, but I have regained it by allowing old habits to creep back in and found myself back in that secure comfort zone again. I'm sure this has happened to many of you. It's hard then to start over again. Nevertheless, remember the feeling you got when you did, then maybe it will help you resume the challenge. One thing's for sure, you cannot go back to the habits that got you into your original position. When you make these life changes, they are changes for the better.

I hope you get something from this book. If nothing else, I just want to share some information I have obtained about health and wellbeing. Maybe it will open your mind and entice you to learn more.

CHAPTER ONE

Obesity

Obesity is a common nutritional disorder. It is excessive fat build-up in the body that can be detrimental to your health. When we hear the word *obesity*, probably the first thing that comes to mind is the food we eat and drink. So let's take a look at our food patterns over the past forty to fifty years.

There has been an enormous rise in obesity since the seventies. There are many reasons for this, one of which is the food we eat. Typically, this food comprises refined carbohydrates and a combination of non-essential fats such as hydrogenated and trans fats. These foods tend to stimulate your appetite and you will probably find yourself wanting to eat more of them. Alcohol also encourages fat storage and many alcoholic beverages contain sugar and provide no nutritional value.

In the seventies, there were abundant harvests of corn in the USA and some of the surpluses were used to make cheap sweeteners such as high-fructose corn syrup. This corn syrup was less expensive than sugar and found its way into many foods and drinks.

Also in the seventies, advertisers in England introduced the idea of snacking between meals with a sugary treat, using advertising slogans like "A Milky Way – the treat you can eat between meals without ruining your appetite" or "A finger of Fudge is just enough to give your kids a treat." For many people, these sugary snacks became a regular part of their daily diet.

We were also exposed to fast food restaurants, then value meals. Further down the line came supersize meals and drinks. Even the Yorkie changed the size of chocolate bars. In addition we had the creation of low-fat dishes. Authorities decided that fat in our diet was a health issue. Many foods had the fat removed. Since fat gave flavour to our food, something else had to be added to counteract this. That ingredient was sugar. Therefore, any benefit you thought you were gaining for your health because of lower levels of fat was cancelled out by the addition of sugar.

When it comes to your food, some of the major contributing factors in the rise of obesity today have been high-fructose corn syrup, snacking between meals with sugary, high-fat snacks, fast food outlets, low-fat dishes and fizzy drinks.

All of these foods and drinks are very pleasant in taste and when you are consuming them, they light up signals of pleasure in your brain. For this reason, some people can find them difficult to resist and often find themselves overindulging in them.

In the last forty to fifty years, we have seen a rise in

obesity to the point where it has gotten out of control. While food and beverages have had a significant impact on this, there's a lot more to it than that.

Factors affecting food choices:

- » Biological – hunger, satisfaction, taste and smell
- » Economic – income and food cost
- » Social – social class and cultural influences
- » Psychological – stress, mood, guilt
- » Individual – beliefs, behaviours, knowledge, attitudes
- » Advertising
- » Environment

Some factors contributing to obesity:

- » Quantity of food/portion sizes
- » Quality/type of food
- » Lack of exercise
- » Lack of sleep
- » Psychological factors, depression, low self-esteem
- » Stress levels
- » Your behaviours and habits
- » Self-talk – what you tell yourself
- » Genes
- » Menopause, due to hormone changes
- » Certain medications
- » Thyroid abnormalities
- » Advertisements
- » Environment

Food Addiction

Food addiction may also be a contributing factor to obesity. Food addiction can be considered an unhealthy relationship with food, typically with foods that are high in fat and sugar. These foods are very pleasurable in taste, triggering the brain's reward system, where you experience pleasure (dopamine effect). As a consequence, some people may find these foods challenging to resist. Some common examples of these are:

- » Sweets, cakes, biscuits, pastries
- » Crisps, peanuts
- » Processed foods, chips, fried food, sausage rolls
- » White bread, rolls
- » Cheese
- » Fizzy drinks

Symptoms experienced with food addiction can include:

- » Overindulging, despite the risks of developing health complications.
- » Eating past feeling full or eating when not hungry.
- » Emotional issues – guilt, unhappiness, anxiety, mood swings.
- » Embarrassment about your eating habits. Hiding what you eat.
- » Lack of enthusiasm for everyday routines or social or family occasions.
- » A decrease in the satisfaction you get from certain foods.

» Increased cravings for particular foods when trying to cut down or eliminate them from your diet. These cravings may be intensified in response to food cues in your environment and advertisements, together with taste and smell.

Here are some steps towards helping with food addiction:

» Eat high volumes of low-glycaemic index (GI) foods. Eat more fruit and vegetables and choose brown rather than white, when it comes to bread, rice and pasta.
» Manage your environment. Remove the food items that trigger cravings, as this will help reduce food accessibility and temptation.
» When doing the shopping, avoid the aisles with food you have difficulty resisting. If you struggle with this maybe you could try shopping online.
» Some people may need to reduce meal frequency. If you eat large volumes of food at a sitting, you could look at eating just three meals a day with no snacking in between.
» Reduce the variety of food choices. Too much choice can make it difficult to reduce temptation and calorie intake.
» Implement behavioural changes – install new healthier habits.
» Keep a food diary, as this will give you an insight into what, when, where and why you eat these "reactive" foods.

There is a theory that when you eat a particular

food regularly, you may become uninterested in it. Unfortunately, this doesn't seem to be the case when it comes to one ingredient, SUGAR. Eating sugar in excess and too frequently tends to intensify the addictive response, encouraging you to want more.

Sugar addiction

When you think of the word addiction, you probably think of drugs and alcohol, but some people feel that sugar has the same effect. Just like drugs and alcohol, when you frequently consume too much sugar, it overactivates your brain's reward system, where dopamine works. If you repeatedly stimulate your reward system with sugar-laden foods, you can get used to them. The receptors for the dopamine signal slow down, reducing the pleasurable feelings. To get back these pleasurable feelings, you have to eat more of these types of foods. This process has a significant effect on your ability to curb that sweet tooth.

To help control your love of sugar, you need to lessen your insulin response. Increasing your intake of fibre and low-GI foods can help decrease your desire for sugary food and reduce your insulin spikes. Adding protein to a meal can also help, as it reduces the rate at which carbohydrates are digested. Reduce excessive alcohol consumption as this will help lessen cravings the next day. Learn ways to reduce your stress levels and get enough sleep.

At the end of the day, nobody chooses to be fat or obese. It's very difficult to control your food intake and lose weight when you are addicted or continuously exposed to certain foods on a regular basis.

Some of the potential implications of obesity:

- » Cardiovascular disease
- » Type 2 diabetes
- » High cholesterol
- » Hypertension (high blood pressure)
- » Psychological issues, depression
- » Pancreatitis, gallstones
- » Female disorders – abnormal periods, infertility
- » Arthritis
- » Gout
- » Kidney stones
- » Liver disease (fatty liver)
- » Asthma
- » Sleep apnea, snoring
- » Certain cancers

Cardiovascular disease

Cardiovascular disease (CVD) is a group of disorders of the heart (cardio) and blood vessels (vascular). It is caused when blood flow to the heart reduces due to a blood clot or plaque build-up. Types of CVD are coronary heart/artery disease, stroke and peripheral vascular disease.

Coronary heart disease occurs when the flow of blood to your heart is blocked or reduced from the build-up of plaque (atherosclerosis), which can cause chest pain (angina) or a heart attack.

A stroke occurs when the blood supply to part of the brain is cut off by a blood clot.

Peripheral vascular disease occurs when there is a blockage in the arteries to your limbs, usually the legs.

Risk factors contributing to CVD:

> » High cholesterol
> » Hypertension
> » Type 2 diabetes
> » High triglycerides (fat)
> » Being overweight or obese
> » Sedentary lifestyle, lack of exercise
> » Family history
> » Excessive alcohol consumption
> » Smoking
> » Stress

How to help prevent CVD:

Eat a healthy diet, reduce your alcohol consumption, lose weight, exercise regularly, reduce stress and stop smoking.

Diabetes

Insulin, which is produced by your pancreas, regulates the blood sugar levels in your body. Without it, your cells cannot absorb glucose (sugar), which they need to produce energy. Diabetes occurs when your pancreas does not create any or enough insulin or when your cells cannot absorb the insulin that it produces.

Symptoms of diabetes:

- » Frequent urination
- » Excessive thirst
- » Increased hunger
- » Fatigue
- » Unexplained weight loss
- » Irritability, mood swings
- » Blurred vision
- » Slow-healing wounds

There are two main types of diabetes:

Type 1 – Insulin dependent (you have to inject yourself with insulin)

Type 1 diabetes occurs when your body cannot produce insulin, as your immune system has destroyed the insulin-producing cells in your pancreas. Type 1 usually develops in childhood or early adolescence but can occur in later years.

Risk factors:

- » Family history/genetics
- » Age

Type 2 – Lifestyle (overweight and lack of exercise)

Type 2 diabetes occurs when your body cannot produce enough insulin, or the insulin cannot be used by the cells of your body properly.

Risk factors:

- » Family history

» Age
» Insulin resistance (pre-diabetes): your blood sugar levels are above normal and the cells of your body cannot absorb the sugar from your bloodstream correctly.
» High triglycerides (fat)
» Overweight, especially around the middle
» High blood pressure (hypertension)
» Low HDLs (good cholesterol)

To help prevent or reverse type 2 diabetes, eat a healthy diet, reduce your intake of sugar and high fat foods, exercise regularly and maintain a healthy weight. These are all very important when it comes to fighting against type 2 diabetes but sometimes you may also need prescribed medication.

Do not self-diagnose. Visit your doctor if you suspect you may have diabetes.

Cholesterol

Cholesterol is a waxy, fat-like substance found in your blood. It comes from two sources. The first source comes from your body (blood cholesterol), primarily the liver and the second from your food (dietary cholesterol), mainly animal products, saturated fat and trans fats. Some cholesterol is essential for life as it is needed to make hormones, bile to aid digestion and vitamin D. You only need a small amount and your body makes all you need to carry out these functions.

Cholesterol is transported in and out of your cells by carriers called HDLs and LDLs:

HDLs = High Density Lipoproteins, which is the good cholesterol.

LDLs = Low Density Lipoproteins, which is the bad cholesterol.

When you have too much cholesterol, it causes the build-up of plaque on the walls of your arteries. It disrupts the blood flow in your body and is a contributing factor for developing cardiovascular disease. Your cholesterol reading should be 5 mmol/L or less.

To improve your cholesterol:

> » Eat less saturated fat
> » Avoid trans fats
> » Choose low-fat cooking methods – spray oil, boiling, steaming
> » Choose unsaturated oils – olive oil, rapeseed oil, etc.
> » Trim fat off meat
> » Eat foods rich with Omega 3
> » Increase your soluble fibre
> » Reduce processed foods and sugar
> » Exercise
> » Stop smoking
> » Limit alcohol

Blood Pressure

This is the pressure applied on the walls of your

arteries as your heart pumps blood around your body. It has two readings:

> » Systolic Pressure, which is related to the pressure in your arteries as your heart contracts
> » Diastolic Pressure, which is related to the pressure in your arteries as your heart relaxes

Blood Pressure Table

Systolic	Diastolic	Classification
<90	<60	Low
≤120	≤80	Normal
121–139	81–89	Pre-hypertension
≥140	≥90	Hypertension

Hypertension, another name for high blood pressure, can carry some serious health risks such as heart disease, stroke and liver and kidney damage.

Risk factors relating to hypertension:

> » Family history
> » Too much salt in diet
> » Obesity, overweight
> » Sedentary lifestyle, lack of movement/exercise
> » Excessive alcohol consumption
> » Smoking
> » Stress
> » Age – as we get older the elasticity in our arteries decreases (arteriosclerosis)

To help control or prevent high blood pressure eat a healthy diet, reduce your salt intake, maintain a healthy weight, take regular exercise and manage your stress.

For hypertension and high cholesterol, depending on the severity and your family history, you could need medication.

Here's an easy way to remember which foods you need to reduce or eliminate from your diet to help with obesity:

CRAP *food*

C – Carbonated drinks containing high-fructose corn syrup

R – Refined sugar found in cakes, biscuits, sweets.

A – Artificial sweeteners/flavourings. Found in confectionery products, soft drinks, savoury snacks. (Or, Alcohol – cannot be stored in the body and promotes fat storage.)

P – Processed foods, food altered during preparation. They can contain refined sugar, trans fats, artificial sweeteners and flavourings, e.g. party foods, sausages rolls, deli meats, ready meals.

CHAPTER TWO

Where to Start

We all generally know how to lose weight and feel healthier – we diet and exercise. However, it's not that simple. It's also about knowing and acknowledging you need to change your thoughts and behaviours towards food and exercise. It's about questioning yourself and looking at areas in your life that can help you achieve what you want. The following chapters are designed to help you explore these areas.

- » Your belief system
- » Your fears
- » Your values (what's important to you)
- » Your behaviours
- » Your habits
- » Your actions
- » Your goals
- » Your nutrition
- » Your exercise or lack of it
- » Your self-talk (your positive to negative talk, what you keep saying to yourself)
- » Your emotions and how you handle them

- » Your stress and how you handle it
- » Your sleep (how much you are getting each night)
- » Your hormones
- » Your responsibility (taking responsibility for yourself and not blaming others – are you always making excuses?)
- » Your environment
- » Advertising and how it affects you

It's about you, what you want and finding a way to achieve it. Understanding that you do have choices and being consciously aware of how you react to situations or comments. It's your reaction that will determine how you will end up feeling and then what actions you take in response.

When something happens or something is said that we do not like, we tend to react immediately. What if we stopped and took a look at the situation, then asked ourselves:

- » "Is there any truth in it?" Sometimes the truth hurts. Sometimes other people's opinions or a different way of looking at things can be helpful.
- » Can you do anything about it?
- » Do you want to do anything about it?
- » What's the best way to handle the situation or comment?

For one reason or another, we seem to look for something or somebody else to blame. Why do we allow what other people say and think to affect us in such a negative way? Why do we think our own opinion is not good enough? We look outside ourselves when the answers are within. We all have the capabilities to make good decisions to achieve what we want. As someone wise once said, "If it's to be, it's up to me."

We also like to take the easy way out, the quick fix, whatever takes the least effort. We turn to something sweet or savoury that we think will make us feel better. Maybe take a moment, think about how you're feeling and think of other ways to help you feel better instead of those that will probably make you feel worse.

- » Go for a walk – if you have a dog, take it with you
- » Have a bath with lots of bubbles
- » Listen to music
- » Phone a friend, have a chat, or call around

There are better ways to help yourself than through food. Open your mind. I know it is easier said than done, but it shows that you do have choices and it's what you choose to do, what action you choose to take, that really matters. Eating the sugary or high-fat food may make you feel better there and then, but you will probably end up feeling guilty. "Why did I eat that? I can't even remember what it tasted like, I ate it so fast. I don't even know how much I ate." It's just short-term pleasure, unrewarding mindless eating. You may then feel angry or get upset and possibly end up eating even more.

So today is the day that enough is enough, no

more excuses, no more blaming others or any outside influences. Today is the day you're going to start taking responsibility for yourself, your actions, your feelings, your thoughts and the position you are in right now. You will get out of your comfort zone and achieve what you have always wanted and deserve. A lifestyle that makes you feel good about yourself and the choices you make.

CHAPTER THREE
Belief System

Your belief system is what you believe to be true. It determines your thoughts and behaviours regarding:

» What is good and what is bad
» What is right and what is wrong
» What is true and what is false?
» What you should say and what you shouldn't say
» What you should do and what you shouldn't do
» What you must do and what you mustn't do
» What you will do and what you won't do
» The right way to do it and the wrong way to do it

These personal beliefs control your reactions to every situation or event that happens in your life. They determine whether you feel happiness or sadness, pain or pleasure. They come from influences (family, friends, teachers, colleagues, TV, etc.) you have been exposed to throughout your life.

Inner beliefs:

» People don't take me seriously
» People don't listen to me

- » People don't value my opinion; I don't value my opinion
- » People don't believe in me; I don't believe in me
- » I'm not good enough
- » Good things don't happen to me
- » I don't deserve to be happy
- » It's too complicated, I could never do that
- » I've tried before and it doesn't work
- » I don't have it in me to do what it takes
- » I never carry anything through so why bother?
- » I can't let my guard down
- » I must be perfect in everything I do
- » If I fail it will be devastating, I'll feel worthless, a failure
- » I should feel guilty and blame myself for all my past mistakes
- » My willpower (self-control) never lasts
- » If I achieve my goal something bad might happen

Beliefs about diet/weight loss:

- » It's too difficult
- » Too much effort has to be put in to achieve my goal
- » I'm afraid of change
- » I will feel deprived
- » I don't like healthy food
- » I have to eat foods I don't like because they are healthier or less fattening
- » I have to give up too much
- » I won't be able to have nice things to eat anymore

- » My diet is going to be so boring
- » I can't lose weight
- » I'll never achieve my weight-loss goals
- » I'll never keep it off, I'll probably put it all back on
- » It's not my fault I'm overweight

Beliefs about exercise:

- » It's too difficult
- » It's too complicated
- » I don't know what to do
- » It's too time consuming
- » I don't like exercising
- » Weights make you muscular

Beliefs about nutrition:

- » There is too much information about what's good and what's bad
- » I don't understand it, it keeps changing
- » I don't like cooking
- » I don't know how to cook
- » I don't have time to cook nutritious food
- » It takes too long to cook from scratch

Every success or failure you experience in your life comes from these personal beliefs. If you believe you will never achieve your goal, saying "It's too difficult, I could never do that" or "I'm not good enough," then these are the messages you are sending to your brain and the chances of you accomplishing it will be very slim. The way you talk to yourself is imperative for your success. If you continue with these negative thoughts, they will become deeply embedded in your brain and your habitual behaviours.

You cannot change the past, but you can take control from this day forward. So if your belief system is not working for you, change it. Design a new belief system for what you want to achieve. What would you need to believe to be true to change your current situation? Believing in yourself – that you will succeed – is very important in the process of obtaining what you want. You need to believe it to achieve it. You need to acknowledge it to change it.

A more positive belief system and approach to succeed:

- » I will take it one day at a time
- » I know the power is within me to achieve my goals
- » I am taking full responsibility for my actions
- » I deserve to be happy
- » I am now achieving my ideal weight and I will maintain it
- » I don't have to give up all my favourite foods
- » Not everything has to be perfect
- » I feel so much better when I eat healthy food
- » I have much more energy when I exercise
- » My best is good enough
- » I am good enough

Internal beliefs can give you a positive outcome or a negative outcome in your life. They can motivate you to achieve or hold you back and stop you from reaching your goals. How you feel about yourself and others is what you will live in your thoughts. You're the one that holds these powerful beliefs and they will inevitably affect you and how you live your life.

Positive change needs to begin internally and these changes can be supported with the necessary actions to make it happen. Believe in the positives in yourself, in your ability. You are good enough and you can achieve your goals. Tell yourself, "I have the capabilities to make positive decisions and change my limiting beliefs."

NEVER UNDERESTIMATE THE POWER OF YOUR MIND

Other powerful thoughts and beliefs:

Predicting the future

Negative: Telling yourself you know you won't succeed – "I'll never achieve that" – so you decide, what's the point in trying?

Positive: Tell yourself that no matter what, "I will do what needs to be done and I will succeed."

Comparing

Negative: You compare yourself to others, determining who's richer, more popular, more intelligent, etc.

Positive: Love yourself for who you are. What other people think about you is not as important as what you think about yourself.

Categorising

Negative: Describing yourself in a very negative way – "I'm so boring", "I'm stupid", "I'm a failure". If you keep telling yourself these things, that will become your reality.

Positive: Describe yourself more positively – "I am great company", "I have a lot of knowledge", "I am an achiever".

Self-criticism

Negative: Criticising yourself for not succeeding, telling yourself you're not good enough. Putting yourself down, giving yourself no encouragement to succeed.

Positive: "I can accomplish my goals with structure and self-belief". "I am good enough".

Internal/external influences

Negative: Blaming outside reasons for your situation or internally sabotaging yourself. Holding other people, friends, family, or yourself responsible for you not succeeding.

Positive: It's within your control to succeed, no one else's. Believe in yourself.

Woe is me

Negative: Self-pity, feeling sorry for yourself. Others

have it easy. Things always go right for them, but not for me. "They don't have to work as hard as I do to achieve." The grass is always greener!

Positive: Think about what you are trying to accomplish and visualise yourself achieving it. Then all your effort will be worthwhile.

Polarising

Negative: All or nothing, black or white, good or bad. It's either one way or the other, there's no middle ground, no grey area.

Positive: It's not always one way or the other. Sometimes you might need to look in the middle.

Minimising

Negative: You keep your achievements to yourself, or you belittle something that you have accomplished. You feel people will think you're too cocky, boastful, or arrogant.

Positive: Let people know about your achievements. It's a positive experience to be shared.

Perfection thinking

Negative: Everything has to be perfect, no slip-ups; you have to be the best, there's no room for second best.

Positive: There's no such thing as perfect. Do the best

you can and know that that's good enough. Remember, you learn from mistakes.

Mind reading

Negative: You think you know what others are thinking. If someone doesn't say hello to you, you decide they are ignoring you or don't like you. You determine what that person is thinking and feeling at that moment.

Positive: Don't presume to know. You have no idea what's on their mind at that particular moment or what kind of day they are having.

Control/being right

Negative: You need to be in control all the time. You cannot let your guard down. You need to prove your opinions and actions are right.

Positive: Let yourself go. You don't have to be right all the time and you certainly don't have to be perfect. Listen to other people's opinions and views. You might learn something.

Fairness

Negative: You feel aggrieved because your idea of what is fair isn't the same as other people's. "They never do anything for me."

Positive: If you want to do something for somebody, do it because you want to, not in the hope of getting something in return. However, if you feel you are being taken advantage of, you could address this with whoever has made you feel this way.

CHAPTER FOUR

Happiness

Happiness is a state of mind. It is something we all want to experience, a feeling of contentment and a peaceful mind. When we think about happiness, many people believe that various things have to happen or be achieved in order to feel happy. Maybe you think you have to be the best at everything you do. Perhaps you need to be liked, appreciated, or respected. Maybe you feel you have to drive a new car, own a big house, have a great job, or even have lots of money.

The fact is, none of the above has to happen for you to feel happy. If you have intense rules about what has to happen before you feel happy, you may be waiting a long time. "When I lose two stone, then I'll be happy", "When I have the perfect body". Waiting for future happiness can stop you from feeling happy right now.

Happiness is a choice. It's in your control. However, you need to take action to achieve it and the same applies if you want to lose weight and feel healthier. Neither will just happen.

There is a theory that you control 40 percent of

your happiness and the rest comes from your genes and life circumstances. This 40 percent gives you a considerable level of control. We take so many things for granted that we neglect to notice how easy it can be to share and create happiness in a way that has nothing to do with material things. Giving someone a compliment or a hug. Telling someone you love them, that you are proud of them.

You can feel happy right now if you repeatedly tell yourself you feel happy, sending a feel-good message throughout your body. You may think that sounds ridiculous, but try it. You might be pleasantly surprised.

Explore areas in your life to enhance your happiness, such as:

Self-esteem

It's all about your perceptions. You are not born with low self-esteem; it is something learned. Most low self-esteem comes from outside influence. Either someone has said something to you, or you have experienced something, maybe even as far back as your childhood.

When someone does or says something to upset you, you will more than likely take it personally and react with a negative response, e.g. go to the goody press (we never seem to go to the fruit bowl). You feel hurt because that's not how you would have treated that person. You need to accept that that's their personality and you cannot change or control it. However, you can manage your response. You could let them know that they have hurt you, or if you find you are unable to do that, learn to let it go (forgive) and move on.

People do and say things for all kinds of reasons. Maybe they are jealous of you and what you may have or stand for. Perhaps they are going through a bad patch themselves and are just lashing out. I'm not saying that's acceptable, but it's up to you how you choose to respond. Stop and think first. If it's really their issue, leave it with them. If it's something you want to do something about, then do. Don't allow anyone else to take away your power. It's your choice.

Find where this low self-esteem originated. What event occurred or who said or did something to cause it? There's only one person responsible for your life and that's you. It's up to you how you live it and how you are treated. You owe it to yourself to be your own best friend, realising what a great person you are.

What's your part in your self-esteem? When you look in the mirror, what do you see? Write it down and then show it to someone. Get them to read it back to you. Then ask yourself, would what you have said be acceptable if someone else said it about you? Would you say those things or talk like that to anyone else? Be very careful with words as they have a huge impact on your happiness and how you feel.

Ask someone you know who loves you unconditionally to write down what they think about you. When you read it, really take notice of what they say and accept it as truth.

It's time to stop beating yourself up or listening to other people's negative opinions. If your unhappiness is to do with another person's point of view or opinion of you, then it's time to challenge it and change it.

Friends

We all have friends that affect us in various ways. Some are always there for you and support you through everything, no matter what. Others make you feel good. You have a great laugh when you are with them and you come away feeling happy. Then there are the ones that drain your energy. You feel you have to psych yourself up before you talk or meet up with them.

Think about your friends. Decide which ones support you, which ones make you feel good and which ones drag you down. Then think about how you are going to continue your friendship with them. You may realise you want or need to spend more time with some and less with others.

Health

Your health and wellbeing are essential when it comes to your happiness. When you feel healthy, you have more energy and you feel better about yourself and the opposite applies when you don't. If you think you could be healthier, either physically or mentally, or both, then find ways to achieve it.

Communication

Lack of communication can cause a lot of unhappiness in relationships. Tell your family and friends what you are trying to accomplish and how they can help. Don't just expect them to know. They cannot read your mind. Let them know how they can support you. Don't use the excuse, "If you loved me, you'd know".

Emotions

Your emotions trigger your feelings and thoughts, which will then determine your behaviour, which will probably make you feel more of the emotion and the cycle continues. You need to become aware of your emotions and when they show up. Acknowledge them and try to understand and learn from them. Keep a diary. Track your emotions, the way you're feeling and the actions you take because of them.

Fear

Don't be afraid to get out of your comfort zone and try new things. Fear is a natural and necessary human emotion. Don't let fear stand in the way of your happiness. Use it as a source of motivation. No matter what happens, the majority of the time, it's fixable. Any failure or setback is a learning experience that can be used as knowledge in the future.

Gratitude

One of the most significant contributors to your happiness is gratitude. It's a powerful way to focus on the positives. We take a lot of things for granted, from the roof over our head, to food on the table, someone doing our washing and ironing, the people that support us, the sun shining knowing it puts us in a better mood and the list goes on and on. We don't seem to think about the simple things or what we have, just what we don't have. Think about it. Look at what you have and be grateful. Grateful people tend to be happier.

Write down what you are grateful for and why. Do this regularly.

Goal setting

There are situations you may experience in your life, such as losing a loved one, losing your job or the breakup of a relationship. These are very upsetting and challenging times. Some people will feel they can't handle what has happened while others find that they can.

How you deal with any setback that you come up against is so important when it comes to your happiness. You don't stop feeling happy because of what's happened to you. It is because of your inability to cope with it. This is when goal setting is essential. Setting goals can help you get back on track. You have to dig deep to get back up when you suffer a setback. Set daily, weekly and long-term goals. This will help you regain control.

Smiling and laughing

Happiness and positivity are infectious, as are sadness and negativity. Surround yourself with people that make you feel happy and good about yourself. Do what makes you smile and laugh more. What your face is expressing and what your body is feeling is sending a message to your brain. Make it a positive one.

Relationships

Build up the positives in your relationships with others. No matter how small, they will help to offset the negatives. Say thanks for the coffee, cleaning the house, bringing the dog for a walk, doing the shopping, etc. They may seem like small gestures, but they go a long way in building up the positives in any relationship. If you don't notice them, they won't register in your mind: gratitude and respect are important.

Nature

Being outdoors and embracing nature can enhance your mood and make you feel happy. Get outdoors. Nature holds a lot of beauty and calmness.

Acts of kindness

Passing on an act of kindness is very rewarding. Not only does it make someone else feel happy, but it also activates the reward area in your brain, so you will also reap the benefits. Acts of kindness include paying someone a compliment, holding the door open for someone, visiting someone who is lonely or living on their own or lending a listening ear. There are many acts of kindness you can do. Try performing some acts of kindness every day.

You are in control of your happiness, so focus on the good things in your life. They say happiness is in the simplest things. Do whatever makes you feel happy.

CHAPTER FIVE

Emotions

E motions are there to support you and help you navigate your life. They are associated with your feelings, thoughts and behavioural responses. They are action signals trying to guide you to a better quality of life, encouraging you to change the way you think and perceive things.

When it comes to your health and wellbeing, eating certain foods is sometimes triggered by emotions or situations (people, places, events). Discover what your triggers are:

- » Good or bad mood
- » Something has happened to upset you
- » Somebody has done or said something to upset you
- » Visiting friends
- » Travelling
- » Being surrounded by tempting food or drink
- » Entertaining friends or celebrating a special occasion
- » Feeling physically or emotionally tired
- » Going to a supermarket, bakery, or sweet shop

» Going to the cinema, a wedding, or a sports game
» Watching TV
» Being surrounded by people who are eating or drinking

To change your relationship with food, you need to become aware and take notice of all your triggers and processes when it comes to your food choices. Before you eat, check how hungry you are, where you are and how you're feeling. This will help you to eat in response to hunger rather than emotion. When we are feeling down or depressed, we often do not notice what we have eaten or how it tasted. It is, therefore, imperative to eat consciously, rather than automatically or out of habit. Enjoy the whole experience you can get when eating food, the taste, aroma and pleasure.

Identify the moods that lead you to overeat and acknowledge how you feel at the time. Mindless eating is not going to solve any issues you are having or benefit your overall wellbeing.

Actions that can help to resolve emotional pain:

» Stop criticising yourself
» Stop listening to others' negativity
» Stop fixating on what other people think, it's what you think that matters
» Believe in yourself, take your own advice
» Forgiveness
» Compassion
» Gratitude

» Acceptance – accept people for who they are, not who you want them to be

Natural and unnatural emotions

Emotions can be categorised as either *natural* or *unnatural*. For example:

Grief – Chronic Depression
Anger – Rage
Envy – Jealousy
Fear – Panic
Love – Possessiveness

Grief: Natural emotion, it allows you to say goodbye when you have suffered a loss. When you express your grief you get rid of it. Grief that is continually repressed becomes **chronic depression**, an unnatural emotion.

Anger: Natural emotion, it allows you to say "no, thank you". It's a protective response to a hurt or threat. Anger that is continually repressed becomes **rage**, an unnatural emotion.

Envy: Natural emotion, makes you wish for something. It encourages you to try harder, to succeed. It's healthy to be envious. Envy that is continually repressed becomes **jealousy**, an unnatural emotion.

Fear: Natural emotion, it builds in a bit of caution. It keeps your body alive. Fear that is continually repressed becomes **panic**, an unnatural emotion.

Love: Natural emotion, that is unconditional, with no limitations or embarrassment, normal and natural love.

Love that is wrapped in rules and conditions, restricted or limited is unnatural love. Love that is continually repressed becomes **possessiveness**, an unnatural emotion.

People deal with emotions in different ways. It appears that people look at either avoiding or denying emotions or acknowledging them in a positive or negative way.

Firstly, avoiding an emotion such as rejection, disappointment and a sense of failure stops you from taking risks. You are reluctant to form relationships or go for particular jobs for fear of people not accepting you or thinking that you're not good enough. By avoiding the emotion, it stops you from probably feeling what you desire most – acceptance, love, respect, happiness. Then you may deny the emotion. You try to camouflage it and pretend it's not happening, but this will only bring more discomfort and pain. Consequently, you may self-medicate with particular types of food, alcohol, or watching too much TV. These are all unhealthy behaviours to escape negative emotions.

Secondly, you indulge your emotions by competing with others and might even pride yourself on being worse off than anyone else. "Life is so much better for them." But when it comes to your emotions, you need to try to understand and learn from them and positively use them. You cannot run or hide from your emotions. Essentially you want your emotions to work for you, not hinder you. Sometimes things may not be as bad as you think.

Get to grips with your emotions

This is not an easy task, but it will be very worthwhile if you do. The following are some ideas that might help you overcome this challenge.

Identify what you feel when you experience an emotion, as this will help you respond to it appropriately. Question your emotion. For example, rejection. Ask yourself, are you feeling rejected, or are you feeling hurt, disappointed, or maybe left out or not taken seriously. Find out exactly what you are feeling when you are experiencing an emotion.

Acknowledge and appreciate your emotions. Do not resist them. They are signals of support to help change the way you perceive something or your actions. They are there to serve you in making a positive change.

Get inquisitive about the message an emotion is sending you. This will help you master your emotion and prevent the same issue from happening again.

Some questions include:

- » What/how do I want to feel?
- » What can I learn from it?
- » What else could it mean?
- » What am I willing to do now, to find a solution?

Another powerful way to handle an emotion is to recall a time when you felt it before and were able to manage it successfully. What did you do to deal with this emotion? Knowing you managed it will help build your confidence because if you have handled it in the past, you can handle it today and in the future. Take comfort in the fact that you know you can handle this emotion.

The best time to handle any emotion is when you first begin to feel it. Ask yourself, "What can I do, right now, to handle this?" Your first answer will probably be "nothing", but if you keep asking, you will eventually come up with a solution.

It's really important not to ignore your emotions. Remember, they are a call to action. When you experience an emotion, experience it. It's your response to the feeling that matters. The more you improve on your negative emotions, decreasing your anxiety and stress, the more it will help you live a more productive and happier life. Find the message your emotions are sending you.

REMEMBER THE SOURCE OF YOUR EMOTIONS IS YOU

CHAPTER SIX
Fear

Fear is one of your natural emotions. It is possibly the one that demands the most significant consideration when it comes to achieving your goals. We are born with only two fears: loud noises and heights/falling. All other fears are learned fears (such as fear of the dark or confined spaces) formed by your belief systems, family traits and life experiences. Some fears are very challenging and are sometimes challenges you will have no control over, such as losing a loved one. However, there are many fears you experience that you can control.

Fears people typically have are: change, new beginnings, dying, being alone, a disappointment, loss of image, failure, being judged, disapproval, rejection, inability to handle a situation, or whatever life throws at you.

Fears that just happen that you have no control over: aging, losing a loved one, accidents, children leaving home, some illnesses, losing a job.

Fears that require you to take action: changing jobs, making friends, losing weight, interviewing, using the telephone, public speaking, making a mistake (so you don't take the chance), making a fool of yourself.

Feelings are always behind the thoughts and responses, helping you to avoid what you fear and need to confront. Automatically, you try to run away from the thought that scares you and you do something to prevent the outcome. However, resisting the fear only empowers it. It affects your confidence and can stop you from doing or accomplishing what you want. Fear shows a lack of trust in your ability to succeed or handle difficult situations you may encounter.

Reduce your fear and develop more trust in your ability to handle whatever comes your way. The need to control every situation's outcome will keep you from making changes or attempting new challenges. What you need to do to change any situation is to change the way you think about it. If you want something badly enough, there is almost always a way to get it.

There is no doubt you will make mistakes along the way, but this is not to be feared as lessons will be learned. If you try something and it doesn't work, then you will know one way not to do it. It's about doing the best you can and knowing that that's good enough. Each time you let go of your fears by taking action, the power of the fear will decrease.

When you get better at recognising your fears, you will be able to identify the thought or thoughts that are your triggers (to overeat). Keep tuning into your thoughts. As you gain awareness, you will be able to release fear whenever it appears.

States of mind to help you manage your fears

These are the moods that determine your power to think, feel and act in a particular way.

Being present

The more you can recognise and not ignore when you have negative thoughts, feelings, or behaviours, the more you will be able to overcome them the moment they arise. Focus on what is happening now, not something else. Live in the moment – practise mindfulness.

Acceptance

Being open-minded and flexible in accepting new opportunities and embracing each one as it presents itself. It's about recognising the positives in each situation.

Inner strength

Standing up for yourself and having the courage of your convictions. When you have something to say, you speak up.

Centred

Looking inside yourself for the answers, knowing you have the confidence and the ability to do so.

Empowered

Having trust in yourself. You are capable and strong

and you know your limits. When you feel empowered, you do what needs doing.

Detached

Not taking things personally, so no blame, shame, or guilt. Being objective with no attachment to what's right or wrong.

Energised

Feeling full of energy to tackle the day ahead, not tired and lacklustre from the start.

Satisfaction

Feeling satisfied that you can do what needs to be done. You have no issue taking the next step, building confidence and courage.

Synchronicity

You accomplish what's before you without stress, strain, or sacrifice. The fear is gone.

Abundance

Not being afraid to share your ideas and resources, your support and love. Knowing there will be plenty in return.

CHAPTER SEVEN

Hormones

Hormones are your body's chemical messengers. They travel in your bloodstream to your organs and tissues and assist in various bodily functions and procedures. Hormones are primarily produced by glands and affect us in many ways, such as growth, metabolism, reproduction, body temperature, sleep, stress, feelings and behaviours.

When it comes to your nutrition, every food you eat interacts with you hormonally. Insulin, leptin and cortisol are three such hormones.

Insulin: your fat-storage hormone that controls sugar in your blood.

Leptin: your fat-release hormone and regulator of appetite.

Cortisol: better known as your stress hormone.

Insulin

Insulin is a hormone made in your pancreas. Insulin prevents the blood sugar levels in your body from getting too high or too low. It helps balance them out, keeping them in a healthy range.

When you eat carbohydrates, your blood sugar rises. When this happens, your pancreas releases insulin into your bloodstream. One function of insulin is to get the cells of your liver and muscles to absorb the sugar from your blood. Once the sugar is inside your cells, it is converted into energy for your body to use when it needs it.

If you eat too many refined carbohydrates containing large amounts of sugar, your blood sugar levels will rise significantly and your insulin supply will increase to counteract it. If you have more sugar in your body than your cells need, insulin will transport the excess to your fat cells resulting in fat gain. The excess insulin is then followed by a sugar low, making you feel tired, agitated and craving more sugary food. It becomes a vicious circle.

Basically, high insulin levels on a regular basis promote fat gain and cravings, so keeping your insulin levels from spiking is key when it comes to controlling your weight.

To promote good sugar levels:

» Reduce sugar and refined carbohydrates (sweets, cakes, processed food, etc.)
» Reduce fizzy drinks
» Eat good carbohydrates and protein
» Eat more high-fibre foods
» Eat more fruit and vegetables
» Get regular exercise
» Manage your stress

» Get enough sleep

If your body continuously has too much sugar in its bloodstream and your cells cannot use insulin correctly, you could develop insulin resistance followed by type 2 diabetes.

Leptin

Leptin is a hormone produced by your fat cells (adipose tissue). Its primary function is to regulate your food intake and how much energy is stored in your fat cells.

Leptin is carried in your bloodstream. It sends a signal to your brain that controls how much you eat. When you have enough leptin your brain gets the message that you are full and that you have sufficient energy stored for your body to function. If you have low levels of leptin, your brain receives the signal that you are not satisfied and your energy stores are low, signalling you to consume more food.

If you are overweight or obese, you will have high levels of the hormone leptin. As it is made in your fat cells, the more fat in your body, the more leptin you will have. Because of the way leptin is supposed to work, your brain should be getting a signal that you are full and there is plenty of energy stored in your fat cells. When this signal is obstructed, leptin resistance occurs. The leptin cannot get the message through, so your brain thinks that you need more food.

Factors contributing to leptin resistance:

- » High sugar consumption (e.g. high-fructose corn syrup)
- » High insulin levels
- » High triglycerides (fat) levels
- » Overeating
- » High stress levels
- » Lack of sleep

The result is you eat more to feel satisfied and regain the energy that your brain thinks you don't have. Your brain then thinks it should conserve energy, making you feel lethargic. Therefore, when leptin is unable to do its job properly, it leads to increased appetite and reduced motivation to exercise.

To help leptin do its job correctly, avoid processed, high-sugar, high-fat foods. Eat more fibre, exercise and reduce your triglycerides. Manage your stress and get more sleep.

Cortisol

Cortisol, produced in your adrenal gland, is probably best known as your stress hormone. It controls your body's response to stressful situations, but it also regulates many other processes in your body, such as metabolism, insulin levels, blood pressure and immune response. Controlling your cortisol levels is very important when it comes to weight issues and your overall health.

Factors connected to excess cortisol:

» Visceral fat around your internal organs, otherwise known as fat around the middle or belly fat
» Food cravings
» Mood swings
» Disturbed sleep
» Fatigue
» Raised blood pressure
» Heart disease
» Reduced immunity

There are many ways in which you can reduce your stress hormone. Meditation, practising mindfulness, tai chi, yoga and listening to slow/soft music or the waves of the sea are helpful ways to alleviate stress.

Bottom line

The hormones insulin, leptin and cortisol all have a significant impact on your body's ability to control a healthy weight and the recommendations to sustain a normal range for each one are more or less the same:

» Reduce sugar and processed and high-fat foods
» Eat more fibre
» Reduce fizzy drinks
» Reduce your triglycerides (fat)
» Eat good carbohydrates and protein
» Eat more fruit and vegetables
» Exercise, move more
» Manage your stress
» Get enough sleep

CHAPTER EIGHT
Sleep

Sleep is an essential element for losing weight and your overall good health. If you are not getting enough sleep each night, your health and weight goals will be affected.

Insufficient sleep can cause mayhem with your hormones, reduce your energy levels and slow down the fat-burning mechanism in your body. When you get a good night's sleep your muscles get recharged, your energy levels are restored, your hormones are reset and your central nervous system (brain and spinal cord) gets a break, especially if highly stressed.

Lack of sleep can lead to a potential increase in food consumption. Those who are tired can often feel emotional discomfort, making them susceptible to food cravings, especially for sugar-laden and high-fat foods. It heightens your brain's desire to eat and can influence your food choices. Good intentions go out the window and you are more likely to react badly to difficult situations or events.

Some of the benefits of sleep:

- » Recharges the body
- » Boosts mental wellbeing
- » Helps with weight loss
- » Better decision making, especially around food choices
- » Increased energy
- » Decreased stress levels
- » Boosts immunity
- » Helps prevent type 2 diabetes
- » Helps ward off heart disease

Some of the consequences of poor sleep:

- » Stress, increased cortisol
- » Irritability
- » Fatigue, low energy
- » Interferes with hormones
- » Interferes with your thinking and decision making
- » Lack of concentration and focus
- » Slows down fat burning
- » Impact on hunger
- » Increased calorie consumption
- » Cravings for sugar and high-fat foods

Improve the quality and quantity of your sleep. Try to aim for seven or eight hours per night.

Examples of how you can accomplish this:

- » Avoid staying up watching television, being on social media, or playing video games, as you can be losing out on valuable sleep time.

» Keep mobile phones, computers, laptops, etc. away from your bedside as they can stimulate your mind.

» Relax and wind down before bedtime: have a shower or bath, do some deep breathing exercises.

» If possible, buy a good mattress and pillow.

» Block out light coming into your bedroom as this can cause you to wake up early.

» Avoid taking stimulants late at night, e.g. coffee and alcohol.

» Get some physical activity during the day.

Sleep is the foundation of your health. At the end of every day, your body needs to physically and mentally repair to function efficiently. Your brain, every cell, tissue and organ, benefits hugely from a good night's sleep.

CHAPTER NINE

Stress

S tress is the body's way of reacting to a challenge. It is a type of tension that manifests when a person responds to the demands and pressures of life. These pressures can come from work, forced obligations, self-criticism, past regrets, family and friends and other various outside sources. It's a physical and emotional experience and can trigger many negative and automatic reactions.

Types of stress

Worry

Feeling anxious about possible bad events in the future.

Rumination

You continuously think about upsetting situations, focusing on bad feelings and experiences from the past, repeating negative thoughts over and over about the causes and repercussions from past events or conversations.

Acute stress

Short-term stress, meaning it lasts for a short period. This is a psychological response to an event or threat. Acute stress manifests from our internal reactions and abilities to cope with these situations. It can lead to emotional distress.

Chronic stress

Long-term stress lasts for a prolonged period. It's a psychological response to emotional pressures that wear you down. You may find it difficult to see ways out of certain situations. In some cases, it can lead to suicide.

Types of stressors

Normal stressors

Paying bills, commuting, family responsibilities, children, friends, housework, planning dinners, lack of sleep, meeting deadlines, traffic, heat, noise, overcrowding, time management, social occasions.

Major life stressors

Chronic illness or disease, the passing away of a loved one, moving house, losing your job, dealing with a bad boss/client/colleague, tragic accident, relationship issues, planning a holiday or wedding, significant family issues (e.g. a will).

When we are confronted with various situations, it will be our perception of them that will determine what type of stress response it will trigger. Some people have a great ability to cope. Others find it very difficult or are sometimes even unaware they are under stress. Consequently, regular stress can have a significant effect on our health.

Symptoms of stress

Psychological

Depression, irritability, anxiety, reduced concentration, mental confusion, poor judgement, frustration, anger, poor self-esteem, poor memory, mood swings. Your thoughts, mood and behaviour are all affected.

Physical

Heart disease, increased blood pressure, stroke, muscular tension, changes in hormones (higher cortisol levels), suppressed immune system, digestive problems, poor absorption of nutrients, disrupted sleep patterns, insomnia, heart palpitations, fatigue, headaches, weight gain or loss, asthma attacks, panic attacks, skin disorders, hair loss.

When it comes to food choices, stress can influence eating behaviours and metabolism. When stressed, you may self-medicate with comfort food containing high levels of sugar and fat. You reach for these foods to make yourself feel better, which they may do in the short term, but in the long term they have a negative effect on your mind (guilt) and body (abdominal fat). Subsequently, you are less likely to want to exercise or put effort into your food preparation. Emotional eating is a coping mechanism for stress and negative feelings, so you need to look at alternative ways to relieve them. The more you improve on decreasing your stress levels, the more it will help you lose fat and feel better.

Stress management

Ways to help manage your stress:

- » Meditation
- » Mindfulness
- » Breathing exercises
- » Exercise
- » Music
- » Massage
- » Baths
- » Laughter
- » Keeping a diary

Meditation

Meditation is a technique for relaxing your mind. It's a method for training your mind to be silent, calming yourself and letting go. It can change your brain's structure and reduce your stress levels and your stress hormone, cortisol. It may help with depression, anxiety and pain. Examples of meditation are mindfulness and breathing exercises.

Mindfulness

Mindfulness is a practice of paying attention, focusing

on what is happening right now in a non-judgemental way and believing there is no right or wrong way to think and feel. It's about your ability to be in the moment. To be fully present and aware of where you are, what you are doing, your thoughts, feelings, bodily sensations and the surrounding environment.

When you are practising mindfulness, your thoughts tune into what you are sensing in the present rather than rehashing the past or imagining the future. Mindfulness can help you to improve emotional stress and cortisol levels. It may also reduce stress eating.

Breathing Exercises

Breathing exercises are an excellent way to help relieve stress and relax your mind and body.

Focus on your breathing. With your mouth closed, take a deep breath in through your nose for a count of four, hold for a second or two and exhale through your mouth for a count of four to eight. Repeat a few times.

When you practise any form of meditation, it is important not to get angry or frustrated if your mind starts to wander and a thought comes into your head. This is normal at the beginning, so don't try to force it out. Let the thought in and then let it go. With practice, your mind wandering will reduce over time.

Physical exercise

Physical exercise is the most underutilised antidepressant. Exercise can reduce stress and help improve your mood. People who exercise tend to experience less mental discomfort and recover faster from stress. Brisk walking, sports, tai chi, yoga and pilates can help reduce negative stress and increase the hormone serotonin, which regulates your mood.

Music

Listening to your favourite music can relax you and make you feel happy. Dancing to it can be just another way to get some fun exercise.

Baths

Having a bath can be a very effective way to relax your body and mind as it gives you some quiet "me time" with no interruptions. Light a few candles.

Massage

Some people don't like getting a massage, but if you do, having one can release tension in your body, making you feel relaxed and calm.

Laughter

Laughing makes you feel happy. It helps to relax you, decreasing your stress hormone and boosts your immune system. Watch a comedy programme or movie or meet up with friends that make you laugh.

Keeping a diary

When it comes to gaining self-control, you need to understand the motives behind your behaviours towards food. Keeping a diary can help you to identify the emotional reasons for your overindulging.

Life is full of challenges that test your ability to manage them. Lack of sleep and stress activates mindless behaviours that can lead to overeating and bad decision making. Getting sufficient sleep and managing your stress plays a big part in controlling your weight and maintaining overall good health.

CHAPTER TEN
Values

Values are what's important to you; your personal rules of behaviour and how you make choices. Basically, they are who you are and how you live your life. The person you become and the actions you take depend on what direction your values have taken you. Whether or not you feel like you're honouring your values is dependent on your rules of behaviour (belief system), which are the triggering devices of your emotions.

When it comes to your goal, the value is the real reason behind the goal you want. Think about what's important to you. Goals are motivated by your values and have to align with them. When taking any action, ask yourself, will it bring you closer to honouring your values or further away? If you make this choice, what values will you have honoured or not honoured?

If your values are health and wellbeing, how are you honouring these values? What is your nutrition like? How active are you? How much exercise do you do? How do you manage your stress? Do you get enough sleep?

If your values are respect and love, how are you honouring them when it comes to yourself? How do you treat yourself?

If one of your values is confidence, what are you doing to honour that value? Do you believe in yourself? What is your self-talk like? Do you do or say things to build your confidence or take it away?

So what are your values? Don't just say something you don't mean because you think it will make you look better to other people. Think about what is important to you. Put them in order of priority. Now see how you are honouring your values. If you find that you are not, ask yourself, what's this about? What's the price you pay for not honouring your values? Maybe unhappiness, frustration, anger, disappointment in yourself. Think about what's stopping you. Maybe you worry about other people's feelings and are afraid of upsetting them or causing an uneasy situation.

Could it be that you don't want to feel a painful emotion? Do you feel that not experiencing a painful emotion is more important to you than experiencing a pleasurable one? Do you find yourself sabotaging your efforts to honour your values, so you do not have to feel this painful emotion? For example, the feeling of rejection. Maybe you will do whatever it takes not to feel this emotion. You won't put yourself in situations where you may be rejected.

The thing is, not wanting to feel this emotion can affect your choices. It can stop you from living by your true values and experiencing the feelings you probably desire most: **success, love, acceptance** and **achievement.**

Examples of values

Health/wellbeing	Acceptance
Happiness	Courage
Love	Self-confidence
Friendship	Adventure
Loyalty	Positivity
Support	Kindness
Honesty	Patience
Appearances	Harmony
Nature	Fun
Strength (physical and emotional)	Knowledge and learning
Rest	Personal growth
Responsibility	Spirituality
Trust	Forgiveness
Security	Relaxation
Wisdom	Pleasure
Success	Compassion
Gratitude	Tolerance
Communication	Independence
Justice	World peace
Commitment	Purpose
Confidentiality	Dignity
Freedom	Fairness

Faith	Generosity
Respect	Creativity
Achievement	Optimism
Calmness	Passion

You may think certain things could be classed as values, but you might be surprised to find that they are not. Values are not something you do or have. They are typically intangible. For instance:

Money is not a value – what it gives you is **fun** and a sense of **security**.

Gardening is not a value – **nature, spirituality** and **calmness** are.

Travel is not a value – **adventure, knowledge** and **learning** are.

When you think of family, it's what you get from your family that are the real values – **love, security, acceptance, friendship, support, loyalty**, etc.

Live your life according to what you value most. When you make choices based on your values, they always lead to a more satisfying outcome. It may not be the easiest choice. It may cause discomfort, or some sacrifices, it may not be enjoyable at times, but it will be the most rewarding.

CHAPTER ELEVEN

Behaviours

Behaviours are actions you take; they are how you conduct yourself. Your thoughts and feelings affect your behaviour. If you can identify the thoughts and feelings that keep you from achievement, you can start to address and challenge them and maybe break the cycle of your behaviour.

The **Stages of Change** model defines the processes of how you can achieve change in behaviours. It gives clarity as to what position you are in when it comes to achieving your goal. Identify which stage of change you are in now and how you can progress. You can exit and re-enter at any stage of the model until you eventually achieve the desired change.

1. Pre-contemplation

At the present moment, you are not considering a change of any kind. You are probably unaware or maybe in denial that some of your behaviours are hindering your health and need to be addressed.

Take responsibility. Become aware of your behaviours. Think about the numerous benefits you will get when you change your unhealthy behaviours.

2. Contemplation

You're thinking about changing your behaviours as you realise they are problematic for your health. You are contemplating the pros and cons of changing and taking action.

Pros: better health, weight loss, looking better, smaller clothes size, more energy, improved mood, confidence, happiness.

Cons: takes commitment, takes effort, too difficult, discomfort, poor mood, too much to give up, takes too long to change, less energy, illness.

While considering change, ask yourself:

>> How would your life be enhanced if you made changes? (Confidence, improved mood)
>> How would your health improve? (Less risk of illness)
>> How would your fitness levels improve? (Increased energy)
>> How would your relationships improve? (Family and friends)
>> How would your view on life improve? (Adventure)
>> What other benefits could you gain? (Weight loss)

3. Preparation

You are ready to take action and intend to do so very soon. You are looking into ways to help you change. For example:

>> How to adopt healthier eating habits and food preparation
>> Exercise strategies
>> Stress-management techniques

This stage helps you identify solutions to barriers that you can do and commit to.

4. Action

You are doing what is necessary to achieve a healthier lifestyle. You have changed old behaviours for new, healthier ones. You are working hard at implementing these new changes to gain a better quality of life.

Tips for staying on track:

>> Monitor your progress – getting results is a great motivator to keep going
>> Reward yourself
>> Review your strategies at regular intervals
>> Get support

5. Maintenance

After about six months, you enter this stage. You continue your commitment to sustain your new lifestyle. You have changed your behaviours for the better and are maintaining them.

In this stage, you need to keep motivated and prevent relapses from occurring. Take a look back at your goals and challenge yourself. Spend more time with those that motivate you to stay on track.

6. *Relapse*

The resumption of old behaviours. Many people have relapsed in their efforts to change and can make numerous attempts to create a permanent behavioural change. It's normal to slip up now and again. This is when you need to dig deep and not give up. Relapses show new barriers have arisen that need to be overcome. Ask for help if you need it.

7. *Termination*

You are not going back to old behaviours. Your health and wellbeing is your way of life now. You're confident that you can manage the changes you have made. You will not go back to old habits as a way of coping.

Barriers that can hinder change:

>> Yourself
>> Negative thinking
>> Past experiences
>> No motivation
>> Lack of confidence
>> Habits
>> Emotional eating
>> Boredom
>> Sleep patterns
>> Stress

- » Lack of knowledge
- » Energy-saving devices like cars, computers, laptops
- » Eating out frequently
- » Variety of different foods
- » Food availability
- » Feeling that only 1–2lbs loss per week is too slow
- » Lack of support

Change is a process, to start you need to know what you want, how much you want it and what you are prepared to do or give up, if necessary, to get it. You need to acknowledge that your behaviours are not serving you well and they need to change. Question yourself and find out what's stopping you from achieving what you want.

Why are you overweight? Perhaps you're addicted to sugar or just food in general. You're unhappy with a relationship you have with a family member or friend. Maybe you struggle with your job or some of the people in your workplace.

Why do you want to lose weight? Maybe to improve your health, feel better about yourself, gain more confidence, have a more attractive appearance, or wear clothes you like instead of just what fits you.

If you have previously lost weight, why have you been unsuccessful at keeping it off? Perhaps you thought that after you lost the weight, you could go back to your old habits, or maybe you put too much pressure on yourself, telling yourself that if you don't reach your ideal weight you will never be happy.

What brings you to overeat? Is it a particular time of the day? Is it combined with activity, e.g. watching TV? When does it happen most? Is it triggered in certain places? Is it driven by emotions: happiness, sadness, or boredom?

Breaking through the barriers

Your urges to eat are triggered by your thoughts and feelings, cravings for particular foods, cues in your environment and specific situations and events. Investigate and audit your day. See when and why you have the urge to have these foods or to overindulge. Find new ways to deal with these urges and be aware of the cues that make you vulnerable as it will help you to prepare to deal with temptation.

Plan and prepare:

- » Set a smart goal
- » Plan meals in advance
- » Make meals in bulk and freeze some
- » Prepare your food the night before if you need to
- » Write a shopping list and stick to it
- » Don't shop hungry
- » What kind of exercise will you do? When and where?
- » What time will you go to bed to get good quality sleep?
- » What techniques will you use to reduce your stress? Try a new sport or get a hobby,

meditate, or practise mindfulness
» If you have to eat out frequently, check the menu before you go. Keep away from the bread basket or, better still, say you don't want any brought to the table

Change your eating behaviours:

» Eat while seated, not on the go
» Eat only when hungry – sometimes you may just be thirsty
» Be in the moment – be consciously aware of what you are eating
» Enjoy your food – take your time
» Do not eat while watching TV – this is mindless eating
» Chew your food well

Track your progress:

» Weigh yourself once a week (only if you want to)
» Body measurements
» The feel of your clothes
» Use a food and exercise diary

Manage your motivation:

» Look at ways to increase your motivation
» Tell friends and family, get support
» Avoid negative thoughts and opinions
» Allow yourself a treat now and again if you want one
» As you lose weight, donate old clothes to charity
» If you have a bad day or week, do not give up,

learn from it and keep moving forward
» Your reason for change needs to be focused on you, nobody else
» You determine your motivation and attitude for success

Reward yourself:

Rewarding yourself is a positive way to encourage you to accomplish your goals. It can give you a sense of success and achievement. You could put money into a jar or savings account every time you lose some weight and then treat yourself (rewards not to be food-based):

» Get a pedicure or manicure
» Have a massage
» Buy yourself something
» Book a weekend away
» When you reach your end goal you should have a large reward.

Change your attitude and adopt a more positive way of thinking:

» Have realistic expectations
» Any weight loss is positive
» Make healthy eating a priority
» Exercise regularly
» Increase sleep quality
» Decrease stress levels
» Be wary of too much focus on a diet and not enough on lifestyle changes

Relapses

Relapses show that new barriers have arisen. If a relapse occurs, it's imperative not to give up and let all the good work you have done so far go to waste. How will you overcome these new barriers? When you have a relapse, learn from it. It's vital for long-term success. Be patient. It will take time to change a lifetime of learned behaviours. However, your brain has an incredible ability to change and thrives on getting new tasks. When you change your behaviour you will retrain your brain.

It's time to take responsibility for your life and stop blaming outside influences, as they will always be there. It's up to you to educate yourself on proper nutrition and a healthy way of life. You need to decide on what you need to do, what habits you need to remove and what ones you need to install. Stop giving yourself permission to eat and do whatever you want, when you want. Sometimes you have to say no. If you don't have time to exercise and plan your meals, maybe your health isn't as valuable to you as the other things you are doing. If you need help, Cognitive Behavioural Therapy (CBT) is currently proving to be a very effective way of achieving successful change.

Cognitive Behavioural Therapy – the talking therapy

CBT: your thoughts; your emotions; your behaviours

» Situation – what triggers the issue?

» Your thoughts – what goes through your head?
» Your emotions – how do you feel?
» Your behaviour – what do you do?
» Your body – physical reactions

CBT helps facilitate change and aids your thought process. It teaches you useful strategies that you can incorporate into your everyday life. It makes sense of overwhelming issues and recognises that thoughts, feelings, physical sensations and actions are interrelated. It helps stop the negative thought cycle, improving how you feel. It doesn't delve into the past as it only deals with current issues. You can use CBT anytime, anywhere, in any situation. It needs full co-operation as no one can change you, you need to do it yourself. CBT is something you may wish to investigate further.

You need to acknowledge and understand why you are the way you are and why you do the things you do. To change, you must become acutely aware of your behaviours, as you cannot change something until you know what needs to be changed.

CHAPTER TWELVE
Habits

A habit is a learned routine of behaviour. It is repeating an action over and over so that it will eventually become automatic and easy to perform. When you do something in a particular way, good or bad, your brain stores it and when you do it regularly, you teach yourself a response that becomes an unconscious association (memory). There are so many learned habits: brushing your teeth, getting dressed, tying your shoelaces and so on. These are habits we don't think about as they happen automatically.

Think of the habits you have built over the years, perhaps eating something sweet every time you have a cup of tea or coffee. Maybe a glass or two of wine every night, a packet of crisps or cheese and crackers, or both. Eating while watching TV. Your habits come down to your routine, what you repeatedly do. When you continue repeating these actions, they can be hard to change. Thus the saying, "Old habits die hard."

To create a new habit takes a bit of time. Doing something once or twice will not be enough. It is said that it takes approximately two months before a new behaviour becomes a habit. However, this is not set in stone as it could take more or less time depending on the behaviour you are trying to install, how difficult it is to perform continuously and you, yourself. I am sure there are many times you have attempted to change your habits towards a healthier lifestyle but without permanent success. Perhaps this is because you think the only way to succeed is to do with how strong your willpower is.

Willpower is the ability to exert self-control. It takes conscious attention and effort, therefore the ability to sustain it is difficult. Willpower will not get you to long-term success as it doesn't last. The challenge of willpower, together with how long it may take to install new behaviours, can make people feel that creating new habits is too difficult to achieve. As a result, they probably give up after a couple of days, or perhaps they are discouraged from even trying in the first place. They tell themselves "it takes too long", "I don't have any willpower", or "why bother, I'll only end up back where I started".

Creating a new habit

The key is to focus on setting up new, healthier habits that will become automatic and easy to maintain. To help you accomplish this, cues in your environment are essential. These are the prompts to remind you to do something, to take action. Another vital element is that of rewards. Rewards can be treating yourself or gaining positive results. When you start seeing results, it encourages you to want to achieve more.

Take a look at the habits you have built over the years towards your food, exercise, sleep patterns and stress management. If your goal is to lose weight and lead a healthier lifestyle, how healthy are they? What can you change? What cues do you need to put in place or remove that will help you succeed?

It is vital to remove any cues that will disrupt your new habits. Get rid of any food in your kitchen cupboards that you find difficult to resist – out of sight, out of mind. Change your environment, so temptation isn't easily accessible.

Don't attempt to change everything at once, as this could be very overwhelming and hard to achieve. Also, make sure what you are trying to install is not too difficult to maintain, as this can cause frustration and disappointment and you might stop trying. Gradually include new habits over time. Start with an easy one and work your way up to more challenging ones. As you see more positive habits becoming part of your daily routine, it will motivate you to keep going.

Which new habit can you install this week that will eventually become part of your daily routine? What cues would you need to put in place to help this happen? For example:

- » Drink one glass of water before meals. I will leave a glass beside the cutlery drawer or buy a water bottle and leave it on the table.
- » Eat more fruit each day. I will leave the fruit bowl in the middle of the table or on the countertop

where it can be easily seen.

» Walk for 30 minutes before breakfast on Monday, Wednesday and Friday. I will leave my runners at the front door or leave my walking clothes where they will be the first things I see when I wake up.
» Go to bed before midnight during the week, get plenty of sleep.
» Practise deep breathing exercises to reduce stress.
» Eat at the table, not in front of the television.

When you feed your brain with more positive actions towards your health and wellbeing, you will feel more content and happier in yourself. Focus on daily routines that will encourage you to replace your old habits with new, healthier ones.

CHAPTER THIRTEEN

Actions

For every action, there is a reaction. You only need one action to get you started on the road to accomplishing your goal. Any kind of action that works towards your goal, no matter how small, will get you there in the end. However, it won't happen overnight. We tend to want things to happen yesterday, but this urgency for results can put a lot of pressure on us. It will take time, so be patient. As you start seeing progress, it will help you to stay motivated.

What actions have you taken today to reach your goal?

Find out what you need to do. Get the information. You need to change what you are doing. We resist change because it might feel uncomfortable or seem like it's too painful. Starting is difficult, but in time, with perseverance, it will get easier.

What actions are you doing now to keep you stuck?

Nobody but you can control what food you eat or what

exercise you are willing to do, the amount of sleep you get, how you manage your stress, etc. There is plenty of help out there if you need it, but ultimately it's down to you. Take personal responsibility.

What do you have to face when you are not taking any action to achieve your goals?

- » Low self-esteem, no confidence
- » Fatigue
- » Anger, anxiety, irritability
- » Unhappiness, discontentment
- » Disappointment in yourself
- » Staying in your comfort zone, so you don't have to take chances and put yourself out there for criticism, fear of failure, or rejection.

What will you gain when you do take action and achieve your goals?

- » More confidence
- » Feeling better about yourself
- » More energy
- » Sense of achievement or success
- » Contentment, satisfaction, happiness
- » Belief in yourself and your capabilities
- » A healthier body
- » A more attractive appearance
- » Smaller clothes size
- » Feeling more sociable

Look at what you gain when you do achieve your goal. It will probably reflect your values more.

Actions to help you gain control

Responsibility

Taking responsibility means understanding that you are accountable for the reactions you give and the choices you make in any given event or situation that happens in your life. It's not about blaming anyone else for anything you are feeling unhappy about or for why you do the things you do or say the things you say. It's about acknowledging that you are responsible for the thoughts and feelings that manifest in your head, that little voice, that destructive self-talk, which makes you put yourself down for past mistakes, not just blaming others, but also blaming yourself for your unhappiness.

It's about taking responsibility for working out what you want, what kind of life you want to live and acknowledging the multiple choices you have when confronted with any experience, situation, or goal you want to achieve.

It is being aware of the signs when you are not taking responsibility, such as anger, blaming others, self-pity, jealousy, being judgemental, feeling impatient, addiction and fatigue. Ultimately, it's about recognising the signs that keep you "stuck".

Start taking responsibility for yourself and the position you are in right now. Stop blaming others, wanting them to be at fault for the way you are. Don't say it's his/her/their fault that you're overweight or have no confidence or self-belief. Acknowledge that you are accountable and you accept the part you have played in your weight situation. Adopt a more positive approach so that you can succeed and are willing to do what it takes. If you don't take responsibility, you will just stay the way you are. Take responsibility.

Self-talk

Self-talk is the constant stream of words that go around in your head. As they are the building blocks for confidence, they can be very damaging or very beneficial to any goal you wish to achieve. Think about what you regularly say to yourself. If your self-talk is negative – "I'll never lose weight" or "it's too difficult to achieve" – these thoughts will be barriers to your success. If your self-talk is positive – "I am losing weight" or "I am obtaining a healthier lifestyle" – these thoughts will enhance your success. Notice your self-talk, the language you use, as self-criticism is very damaging. If your self-talk is very destructive, then your confidence will be low. Increase your confidence with more positive self-talk. You will be a more successful person if you do. "I am", "I can", "I will", "I know."

Examples of some negative to positive self-talk:

I should versus I could

- » "I should" implies pressure, that the choice is not yours and guilt will follow if you don't.
- » "I could" implies the choice is yours. You don't feel obligated to do something.

Not my fault versus totally responsible

» "It's not my fault" implies you are taking no responsibility for yourself. It's always to do with someone else.
» "Totally responsible" implies you acknowledge your actions and are accountable for them.

I hope versus I know

» "I hope" implies feelings of worry and sleepless nights.
» "I know" implies you have the capabilities to handle whatever needs doing.

I can't versus I won't

» "I can't" implies you have no control over something.
» "I won't" implies you have a choice whether to do it or not.

If only versus next time

» "If only" implies regret and missed opportunities.
» "Next time" implies you have learned from the situation and will know what to do in the future.

To help with some stressful thoughts, ask yourself:

» Is it true?
» Am I jumping to conclusions?
» Am I exaggerating?
» How do I know it will happen?
» So what if it does happen?
» Is it really as bad as it seems?
» Is there another way to look at the situation?

Affirmations

These are strong positive statements written in the present tense to help achieve a more positive way of thinking. They are aimed at increasing positive self-talk; repeated daily they will enhance your ability to accomplish your goals. Make your affirmations for what you want. Read them in the morning and before you go to bed. For examples:

- » I am good enough
- » I am in control
- » I have all the answers
- » I am my own best friend
- » I am handling my fears
- » I am becoming more confident every day
- » I love and respect myself
- » I have a lot of love to give
- » I am a good friend
- » I am an interesting person
- » I set and achieve my goals for me
- » I am making healthier food choices
- » I am creating a healthy mind that is full of positivity
- » I am creating a healthy body and a healthy lifestyle
- » I am feeding my brain and body nourishing food to function efficiently
- » I am now 100 percent accountable for my experiences in my life
- » I have the ability within me to make positive choices and change my limiting beliefs

YOUR SELF-TALK/THOUGHTS AND THE LANGUAGE YOU USE POWERFULLY PROGRAM YOU

Facing your fears

What are you afraid of when it comes to reaching your goal? Fears and doubts affect your confidence and your ability to achieve what you want. When you face up to your fears, you will reduce barriers that stand in your way. Let go of past failures and setbacks as they are all learned experiences. Remember, the greatest obstacles in life are typically internal. You fail to improve your health because it's easier to stay the way you are. There is less fear, effort, or discomfort. It's okay to have some fears and doubts as long as they give you the motivation, rather than holding you back and stopping you from achieving your goal.

Motivation

Motivation is what drives you to take action and do something towards accomplishing what you want. You can have internal motivation, which comes from your desire, your motives for success, or external motivation that comes from other people or events. While external motivation is encouraging, self-motivation is more effective and more rewarding when you succeed. It gives you a great sense of achievement.

To stay motivated, you must have a passion for what

you're trying to attain. If you don't have the passion, you won't have the motivation or enthusiasm to achieve it. Look for internal motivation. You have the capabilities inside yourself to accomplish what you want.

There are many ways to get motivated and stay motivated:

- » Personal goal-setting
- » Measuring your progress. Take a photo, take measurements
- » Accessing your fitness
- » Keeping a diary of your achievements
- » Rewarding yourself when you reach a target
- » Visualisation – visualise how you will look when you reach your goal
- » Exercise – makes you feel good and gives you energy
- » Keeping a food intake diary
- » Getting compliments as you progress
- » Getting support from your family and friends
- » After a successful day, write down how you feel and put it somewhere visible; read regularly

Motivation plays a crucial part when it comes to successful change. Find the motivation to accomplish your goal.

Delaying gratification

Delaying gratification is when you delay the instant pleasure you get from certain foods for a much bigger reward in the future (weight loss). When you get the urge to eat something to make you feel better, try and delay eating it by telling yourself you will have it later or at the weekend. By doing this you may find that you will eat less of these foods over time. This process can be very beneficial when it comes to losing weight. It can improve your ability to resist, thereby encouraging success.

Visualisation

Visualisation is a powerful technique that uses your imagination to help you achieve something. It gives your mind a picture of what you are trying to accomplish. The more imagery you can give your mind, the more it has to work with, and the deeper it will imbed into your subconscious.

Visualise your goal. Visualise in your mind what you have to do to get it. Visualise yourself losing 1-2 pounds a week. Visualise the way you would like to look. Visualise yourself wearing the clothes you want to wear. Visualise how good you feel in them. Visualise yourself achieving your ideal weight.

Example of a visualisation exercise:

> » Sit comfortably in a chair and close your eyes. Start to focus on your breathing.
> » Breathe in and out, relaxing your mind and body.
> » Breathing is slow and controlled.
> » Imagine yourself in a happy place, a place where everything is as you would like it to be, maybe in a garden or on a beach, a place where

you feel relaxed. Take note of what's around you, what you see (flowers, trees), what you can hear (birds singing, laughter, waves of the sea) and what you can smell (the air, a perfume).

» Slowly breathe in and out.
» Now turn your focus on yourself, looking at yourself in a mirror. See yourself as a slimmer you, the body you have always wanted, achieving the weight you would like to be. See yourself smiling back at yourself, feeling really happy.
» Visualise how good you look. How much more confidence you have. Focus on the clothes you're wearing, how they look on you, how they make you feel. Admire yourself.
» Breathe in and out.
» Now just sit for a few moments getting comfortable with this new you. Slimmer, more confident, happier, less stressed you. Breathing in and out, feeling fully relaxed.
» Now, slowly come back into the room. Slowly count down from ten to one. Open your eyes, feeling happy and relaxed.

Time management

Managing your time is an essential element to help you get results. Too often, excuses are used, like "I'm too busy", "I don't have the time to cook", "I don't have the time to exercise" and "there are not enough hours in the day". Yet there always seems to be plenty of time to watch TV, be on social media, or go out socialising.

It's about organising yourself and your time the best way you can. Try creating a schedule for your day with dedicated times for activities such as exercise and meal planning. Such a schedule does not have to fill your day but can help to give it some structure. It's difficult to plan or account for every minute of your day, but it's important to create timeslots for certain activities that need to become a part of it. Timeslots that shouldn't be missed, i.e. if you say you are going to go for a walk or do a gym session at 10 am, make sure you stick to your plan and do it.

Those that say they don't have time to exercise or prepare meals will eventually have to make time for illness. It's about deciding what's important to you and putting it into your daily routines.

Excuses, excuses, excuses

» Going out Friday, so I'll start Monday
» Broke it on Tuesday so I'll start next week again
» I'll get started when I come back from holidays
» I'll lose a bit of weight first then I'll join a gym
» I've had a bad day, I need some comfort

The list is endless. Lose the excuses. All these excuses are just keeping you from feeling some discomfort. Changes are going to be tough in the beginning, but don't allow that to stop you. Challenge yourself. It will be very rewarding and worthwhile.

How serious are you about your health and wellbeing? The only thing stopping you is you. Start today, take action, and soon you will see positive results.

CHAPTER FOURTEEN

Goals

A goal is something you want to accomplish, typically a lifestyle change. A goal encourages you to take action and achieve something, which will likely give you a great sense of satisfaction and success.

Objectives of goal setting:

- » Gives clarity to what you are aiming for
- » Creates an action plan
- » Presents a challenge
- » Helps make changes achievable
- » Powerful motivation tool
- » Measures progress
- » Helps reduce obstacles

Your goal must be clear and well defined, so you know precisely what you are trying to achieve and how to achieve it. Make sure you have the knowledge and resources available to you. This way, there will be no misunderstandings. You need to focus on your goal and be fully committed to the process of accomplishing it. Your goal also needs to be challenging. It needs to keep you interested and motivated, but it may cause you to give up if it is too difficult to reach. Therefore, it's good to have regular feedback to see what's going well and what's not and how you can change things if you need to.

Goal setting

The SMART goal formula is an effective way to help you set a goal. When you write your goal down on paper, it gives a clear picture of what you are trying to accomplish.

S = Specific – clear and well defined
M = Measurable – how you will know you have achieved it
A = Achievable – how you accomplish your goal
R = Realistic – is it possible to do, can you achieve it?
T = Timeframe – date to reach a goal

Specific

Write your goal down in as much detail as you can. What you want, why you want it, how you will achieve it, where you will achieve it and who else could be involved. The more you tell your subconscious, the more information it has to work with, thereby giving you a better chance of success. Write your goal using "I am" and "I will" over "I want" and "I would like" statements. I am and I will imply more positive, affirming statements. It's happening!

A goal to exercise more is not specific. A goal

stating that you will walk for 30 minutes four times per week first thing in the morning in the park is. You are declaring what you will do, how long you will do it, when you will do it and where you will do it.

Measurable

Make sure your goal is measurable, otherwise how will you monitor your progress or know you have been successful? Measuring your progress is a great way to see results and keep you on track. If you don't see some improvements, it may be hard to stay motivated and keep going. Measure your progress regularly. You might need or wish to change something.

- » Take body measurements
- » Fitness assessments
- » Weigh-in once a week
- » Take a photograph
- » How your clothes fit
- » Exercise diary
- » Food diary

A goal to eat healthier is not measurable, but a goal of eating 1800 calories a day by keeping a food diary is. You will be able to see what you eat, how much you eat, where you eat and what changes you can make.

Achievable

Identify what you have to do to accomplish your goal. Do you have the capabilities? Your goal ought to be challenging but not so difficult that it becomes unattainable. Have you got enough information and resources available to you?

- » What actions do you need to take?
- » Changes to your diet – how will you do it?
- » Exercise – how often, when, where, for how long?
- » Sufficient sleep – how will you get this?
- » Stress management
- » Time management
- » Do you need assistance?

Realistic

Your goal needs to be realistic. You have to be able to work towards it. You're the only one who can decide how difficult or challenging it should be. Bearing in mind your capabilities, you need to have enough time, knowledge and resources available to you to achieve it. There is no point in committing to something you know is not realistic and will not fit in with your current lifestyle. If you have a lot going on in your life, with work and family commitments, trying to commit to exercising for an hour five to six days a week may be unrealistic. But committing to exercising twice during the week and once at the weekend might be.

Ensure your goal is both realistic and achievable, to keep you on the right road for successful change.

Timeframe

Timeframe refers to the amount of time you will give

yourself to reach your goal. All goals need to have a time limit, otherwise you could be trying to achieve them forever. How long are you going to give yourself? Creating a timeline with some mini-goals within your main goal is an excellent way to help you determine a realistic and suitable timeframe.

I am going to lose two stone and fit into a size 14 dress by 25 December.

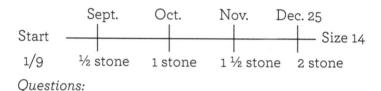

Questions:

- » When?
- » What can I do today?
- » What can I do four/eight weeks from now?
- » What can I do three months from now?

When considering your goal, it must be personal to you. It needs to be consistent with your values and behaviours. Since your behaviours become your habits, it's imperative that they align with what is required of you to reach your goal.

Say your goal is to lose two stone in the next four months to feel healthier, have more energy and finally have control of your wellbeing.

To achieve this goal, you have to know why you want it. What is the emotion behind it? What impact will it have on your life? If you lose the two stone, will it mean you will gain more confidence, look good, get a sense of achievement, feel happier? The emotional reason is fundamental when considering your goal. It will increase your motivation and your chances of success.

Look at your goal:

- » What do you have to do to achieve it?
- » From that list, what are you willing to do?
- » Do you have to give up something?
- » Do you have to include something?
- » What old habits do you need to change?
- » What new habits do you need to implement?

If your present habits consist of eating a lot of sugary and high-fat foods, exercising very little and staying up late either watching TV or being on social media, it's fair to say they will not help you to reach your goal. Your habits need to be in line with what you are trying to achieve. Unless you change them, your chances of succeeding are zero.

Honesty is essential here. There is no point promising to do or give up something that you know will never be sustained. If you do, you may become discouraged and possibly give up. Make a list of what needs to be done. Then make a list of what you're willing to do, what you're willing to include and what you are willing to give up, for example:

- » Smaller portion sizes
- » Reduce sugar intake
- » No butter on the potatoes
- » Trim fat off meat

» Drink more water
» Not drinking alcohol during the week
» Give up a night out
» Watch less television
» Spend less time on social media
» Play fewer video games
» Exercise, move more
» Go to bed early during the week
» Practise mindfulness

Don't overwhelm yourself at the beginning by trying to change everything at once. You only need to change one thing to get you started and then you can move on from there. Have a look at your habits and see which ones need replacing.

To help encourage your success, visualise your goal in your imagination. Give your subconscious a picture of it. Visualise what you have to do. Your subconscious only carries out your instructions. Visualise yourself achieving your goal and how it makes you feel.

It is crucial to establish at the beginning what you need and are willing to do, then there will be no confusion as to what is required of you. It will also help to determine how soon you are likely to accomplish your goal. When you do something, ask yourself – will this action take you closer to reaching your goal or further away? If you find yourself doing something that takes you further away, stop, correct it and carry on. Don't give up, as it's a process – it will be very satisfying when you achieve your goal.

CHAPTER FIFTEEN

Exercise

Physical activity is any body movement that uses energy (burns calories). These activities can include household chores, gardening, playing with the kids, shopping and running around at work. They are part of our daily and weekly routines.

Exercise, on the other hand, is a subcategory of physical activity. It is planned, organised activities aimed at improving physical fitness and health, e.g. going to the gym, training for a sport, exercise class and going for a walk.

Exercise is so important when it comes to our health and wellbeing, yet so many of us struggle to fit it into our day or even our week. This could be to do with our negative self-talk towards exercise. We talk ourselves out of doing any, for whatever our reasons. One of these could be the process of getting started, not the actual exercise itself. It's getting off the couch or out the front door that's the issue. Then there are the excuses: I'm tired, I've had a tough day at work, I'm too busy, it's too time-consuming, to name a few.

Look at the numerous benefits exercise and physical

activity have on your health. Hopefully, this will entice you to include more in your daily/weekly routines.

Physical benefits:

- » Strengthens heart muscle
- » Increases muscle mass
- » Increases basal metabolic rate
- » Improves circulation
- » Healthy lungs
- » Improves energy
- » Aids weight loss and decreases fat around the middle
- » Aids weight maintenance
- » Improves appearance
- » Improves posture

Health benefits:

- » Improves unhealthy cholesterol
- » Helps lower blood pressure
- » Decreases risk of heart disease and stroke
- » Helps osteoporosis, arthritis
- » Reduces high blood sugar levels
- » Reduces high triglycerides (fat)

Psychological benefits:

- » Relieves stress, anxiety
- » Improves mood
- » Helps with mild depression
- » Improves confidence, self-esteem
- » Improves sleep
- » Improves motivation

To inspire you to get active recall a positive memory of an exercise experience that made you feel good. It doesn't matter what you do or how big or small. Doing something is better than doing nothing at all. Make sure what you do is enjoyable, that you have fun doing it, as this will help you to stick with it. If you don't enjoy what you are doing, you won't have the motivation to keep it up. Start making small changes today to get you active:

- » Play a sport you like
- » Exercise with a friend
- » Go for a walk/cycle
- » Join an exercise class or club (a great way to meet people)
- » Dance
- » Music is a great motivator when exercising

There are many changes you can make to increase your daily physical activity:

- » Use the stairs instead of the lift
- » Get off the bus one or two stops early
- » Walk to the shop instead of driving
- » Walk or cycle to work where possible
- » Park your car a bit away from your destination and walk the rest
- » Go for a walk before breakfast or at lunchtime, even for 10-15 minutes
- » Go for a walk with a friend to have your chat instead of using the phone
- » Walk on a treadmill or cycle a stationary bike if you have one while watching TV

Even at home while waiting for the kettle to boil:

Side leg raises, 8–15 repetitions (reps) each leg. Standing up straight, extend right leg out to the side, keeping it straight hold for 1–2 seconds and return to start position. If you can, try not to let your foot touch the floor during each rep. Change leg and repeat.

Squats, 8–15 reps. Stand with your feet shoulder-width apart. Lower body as if you are going to sit into the back of a chair (make sure your knees do not travel over your toes), hold for 1–2 seconds then return to start position.

Standing on one leg, hold for 10 seconds, then change leg. Repeat five times.

Depending on how confident you are at doing these exercises, you can start by holding onto the countertop, then with just your fingertips, then no hands.

Watching the TV during the ads:

Stand up, sit down, 15–30 seconds (holding on to the arm of the chair or hands-free).

Walk or run up and down the stairs.

Shoulder rotations, gentle circular movements. Either standing up or sitting down, hands by your side. Raise shoulders slowly up towards your ears (don't tense up), then backwards, downwards, forwards and back to start position. Then change direction. Do three to five times each direction.

Heel/toe raises, 30 seconds. Feet flat on floor. Raise heels, hold for one or two seconds and back down. Raise toes, hold for one or two seconds and back down.

Your body needs energy (calories) to exercise and function properly; the following explains the processes involved:

Metabolism: This is the chemical processes used by your body to convert what you eat and drink into energy to maintain life.

Metabolic Rate: This is the rate your body uses energy (burns calories, a calorie is a unit of energy).

Basal Metabolic Rate: This is the rate your body burns calories on essential bodily functions during rest and sleep. Such functions include your heartbeat, breathing, body temperature and blood circulation.

You can speed up your fat loss by increasing your basal metabolic rate through regular exercise and increasing your muscle mass.

The three primary fuels for exercise are carbohydrates, fats and proteins.

Fast: carbohydrates (carbs) as fuel
Slow and easy: fats as fuel
Depleted carbs and fats: proteins as fuel

When you exercise, there are different training zones that you can use. Each zone is based on a percentage of your maximum heart rate (MHR). What zone you train in depends on what you are trying to achieve: fitness, weight loss, etc. The basic formula for your maximum heart rate is 220 minus your age. If you are aged 50, you subtract 50 from 220, which is 170. If you want to train in the aerobic training zone, you multiply 170 by 70 to 80 percent and this gives you the heartbeat range at which to work (119–136).

Training zones:

Endurance/Easy	50% to 60% MHR
Slow Long Distance/ Medium Effort	60% to 70% MHR
Aerobic Zone/Hard	70% to 80% MHR
Anaerobic Zone/Very Hard	80% to 90% MHR
Extremely Hard	90% to 100% MHR

When you exercise, you burn calories to fuel your muscles and no matter what training zone you are working at, you will always be burning calories. The level at which you do this depends on the energy system you are using.

Energy Systems:

Aerobic (with oxygen) is continuously exercising using oxygen at a rate where the body can replenish it inside the working muscles, e.g. running, walking, cycling, rowing.

Anaerobic (without oxygen) is exercising where oxygen is used up quicker than the body can replenish it inside the working muscle. Therefore, it's challenging to keep it up without rest periods, e.g. sprints, power lifts, burpees, star jumps, an all-out effort for short periods. (Anaerobic exercise only uses carbs as fuel.)

It is recommended that you do 150 minutes of moderate activity or 75 minutes of vigorous activity plus two muscle strengthening days per week.

- » Moderate activity/exercise (50% to 70% MHR) increases your heart rate, causes you to breathe harder than normal, but still allows you to hold a conversation.
- » Vigorous activity/exercise (70%t to 90% MHR) increases your heart rate, causes you to breathe more rapidly, making it difficult for you to hold a conversation.
- » Resistance training strengthens your muscles and posture.
- » Always work to your capabilities.

Examples of moderate activity/exercise:

- » Brisk walking
- » Cycling (12–14mph/19–22km/h)
- » Doubles tennis
- » Volleyball
- » Aqua aerobics
- » Skateboarding
- » Cleaning – washing windows, vacuuming
- » Mowing lawn – push lawnmower
- » Dancing

Examples of vigorous activity/exercise:

» Jogging/running
» Cycling (14–16mph/22–26km/h)
» Skipping
» Aerobics
» Circuits
» Gymnastics
» Hockey
» Singles tennis
» Rugby
» Football
» Basketball
» Martial arts
» Swimming

Examples of muscle strengthening:

» Resistance training
» Lifting weights
» Resistance bands
» Using your own body weight, e.g. press-ups
» Yoga, tai chi, Pilates
» Sports such as gymnastics
» Manual labour

Plan and prepare 5 "W"s and 1 "H" to exercise

WHY: Why do you want to exercise? To lose weight, get fit, improve your physique.

WHO: Who will exercise with you? With a friend, with a group or class, or on your own.

WHAT: What kind of exercise will you do? Walking, cycling, dancing, aerobics, a sport. Make sure it's something you enjoy.

WHERE: Where will you do it? At the gym, in the park, at home, leisure centre, sports grounds.

WHEN: When will you do it? Before or after work, before breakfast, on your lunch break, in the evening, at the weekend.

HOW: How can you realistically fit it into your lifestyle?

Types of training

Cardiovascular (cardio, CV) training is any form of continuous exercise that strengthens the ability of the heart and lungs to carry oxygen to working muscles.

Benefits:

» Strengthens the heart and lungs
» Improves circulation
» Aids weight loss/maintenance
» Improves sleep
» Improves mood
» Improves stamina
» Decreases resting heart rate
» Improves recovery after training, heart rate returns to a normal rate faster

Types of exercise: running, cycling, walking, rowing, swimming, playing sports, aerobic classes and many more.

Resistance training is a form of exercise that helps to increase your muscle strength and endurance. It is exercising your muscles using an outside force to make them contract.

Some people completely dismiss this type of training for fear of getting too muscular, especially females, but that is not the case. This form of exercise, done correctly, is very effective for fat loss and overall health. The more muscle you have, the more calories you burn, as you need more calories to move muscle than you do fat.

Benefits:

- » Changes in body composition – increased muscle to fat ratio
- » Improves muscle strength, endurance, growth and tone
- » Improved performance in sport
- » Increases basal metabolic rate
- » Assists in weight loss/maintenance
- » Improves appearance
- » Improves sleep
- » Improves posture
- » Less risk of injury
- » Bone health – decreased risk of osteoporosis
- » Improves mobility and balance

Resistance training is performed in sets and reps (repetitions). A **rep** is one completion of an exercise, e.g. one squat, one chest press. The amount of reps you do depends on what you are trying to achieve.

Lower amount of reps = strength training and power

Higher amount of reps = muscular endurance and toning/physique

A **set** is the number of reps you do in one go, for example:

10 reps of squats = 1 set

3 x 10 squats = 3 sets of 10 reps

1 **rep max (RM)** is the most you can lift once in any exercise. Therefore 10 rep max is the most you can lift ten times.

Types of resistance:

- » Free weights/dumbbells/barbells
- » Kettlebells
- » Weight machines
- » Bodyweight
- » Resistance bands
- » Medicine ball
- » Stability/Swiss ball
- » Ankle weights/hand weights
- » Bottles of water, tins of beans

When doing resistance training, technique is so important. You must use a full range of movement and don't lock out your knees and elbows. Engage your abdominal muscles when performing each exercise. Avoid arching your back, tensing/straining your neck, or swaying your body. Let your muscles lift the weight, not momentum. Exhale when lifting the weight and inhale when lowering. If looking for strength and power, the lifting part of the rep is the most important movement. The lowering part of the rep is most important for someone looking for physique (definition/toning) improvements.

There are different types of exercise to work your muscles:

Compound exercises: these exercises aim to target more than one muscle group, e.g. chest press, lunge, squat, shoulder press, lat pulldown, deadlift.

Isolation exercises: these exercises aim to target primarily one muscle group, e.g. bicep curl, triceps extension, leg curl, leg extension.

When designing your programme, it is best not to work the same muscle groups two days in a row as your muscles need time to recover from your workout.

For example:
- » Upper body one day and lower body the next
- » Work legs and back one day. Chest, shoulders and arms the next
- » Alternate between push exercises one day and pull exercises another. Examples of push exercises include chest press, leg press. Pull exercises include lat pulldown, seated row.

How you perform resistance training depends on what you want to accomplish and at what level you are: beginner, intermediate, or advanced. If you have never done this type of training before, it would be advisable to get someone with professional experience to demonstrate how to do it correctly. They can also help you decide which resistance exercises you should do and how many reps and sets for what you want to achieve. For example:

Strength gain – reps 2–8, sets 3–5, rest for 2–5 mins between sets.

Muscle growth – reps 8–12, sets 3–6, rest for 30–90 seconds between sets.

Muscle definition/tone – reps 12–20, sets 2–3, rest for 30–60 seconds between sets.

As you get stronger, challenge yourself. Vary your workouts. Don't keep doing the same thing week in, week out. Change your routine every six to eight weeks.

Exercise of any kind will help you lose weight, but some forms are better than others. Combining cardiovascular and resistance training is very effective for fat loss. An excellent example of this is circuit training.

Circuit training is a sequence of exercises using different components of fitness. You set up a number of stations with a variety of exercises. The exercises are performed one after the other with various rest periods in between. The type of exercise and rest periods depends on what component of fitness you are using. You can do many types of circuits, such as aerobic, anaerobic, resistance, aerobic/resistance, depending on what you want to achieve. For example:

Aerobic circuits: each exercise is performed for 30 or 40 seconds, with 10 seconds of rest in between. If you are at an advanced level, you could have no rest period in between.

Anaerobic circuits: high-intensity type exercises performed for 20 or 30 seconds, with 30 seconds to a minute of rest in between. These circuits would not be advisable for a beginner.

Aerobic and resistance circuits: these combine both components of fitness with a ratio of perhaps 1:1 or 2:1 (two aerobic to one resistance or vice versa). Each exercise is performed for 30 to 40 seconds, with 10 seconds of rest in between. If you are at an advanced level, you could have no rest period in between.

Examples of exercises for circuits

Aerobic exercises:

- » Jumping jacks
- » Strides
- » Knee raise
- » Leg curls
- » Skipping
- » Jogging on spot
- » Side-to-side hops
- » Shuttle run
- » Heel digs

» Jump forward and back (feet together)
» Jump side to side (feet together)
» Pendulum
» Back lunge
» Side lunge

Anaerobic exercises (advanced):

» Burpees
» Mountain climbers
» Tuck jumps
» Star jumps
» Squat thrusts
» Squat jumps
» Power lunge
» Bench jumps
» Double-leg leaping
» Single-leg leaping
» Sprints
» Pyramid sprints

Resistance exercises:

» Chest press, press up
» Squat
» Lunge
» Shoulder press
» Single-arm row
» Prone row
» Plank
» Back extension

There are other forms of exercise classes you could look into that you might enjoy, such as aerobics, step class, kick-boxing, kettlebells, TRX training, aqua aerobics, boot camps, or body conditioning.

Flexibility is the ability of your joints to move freely through a complete range of movement. Your muscles, tendons and ligaments determine the amount of movement you have at each joint. Flexibility is very important for sport and your general wellbeing. It helps you move more freely throughout the day. Still, it is often neglected because people think it's not really necessary.

Benefits:

» Helps prevent muscle injury
» Help prevent muscle imbalances
» Increases agility
» Improves sports and exercise performance
» Improves range of movement and posture
» Helps prevent lower back problems
» Helps with relaxation

Flexibility training consists of exercises that involve stretching your muscles to the point of tension. For instance:

Static stretching involves holding a stretch on a particular muscle (e.g. hamstring) for a number of seconds and then releasing it.

Dynamic stretching involves moving your body through a stretch, e.g. a walking lunge or pulling your knee into your chest for two to three seconds as you step.

There are many classes you can attend that are very

good for your flexibility, such as yoga, pilates and tai chi. Gymnastics is also excellent. In fact, I believe it should be compulsory in junior school, even if just at a basic level.

When it comes down to it, there are many forms of exercise you can choose from. If you can find something you like doing, your ability to continue exercising is greatly increased. Find out what you like doing and do it.

CHAPTER SIXTEEN

Nutrition

Nutrition is fuel for your body and you need proper nutrition for your body to function efficiently. If you consume a lot of unhealthy, sugar-laden and processed foods, it will affect your body's ability to do this. Your essential nutrients are:

Macro-nutrients, macro meaning large, so you need them in large amounts. They are your carbohydrates, proteins and fats.

They provide energy (calories) needed for growth, repair, metabolism and other bodily functions, e.g. your nervous and immune systems.

Carbohydrates provide four calories per gram.
Proteins provide four calories per gram.
Fats provide nine calories per gram.

Micro-nutrients, micro meaning small, so you need them in smaller amounts. They are your vitamins and minerals and are essential for normal bodily functions and good health.

Vitamins

Water-soluble – B group and vitamin C.

Fat-soluble – Vitamins A, D, E and K

Minerals

Major – calcium, magnesium, potassium, sodium, phosphorus, chloride and sulphur.

Trace – iron, zinc, iodine, selenium, copper, manganese, chromium and fluoride.

Benefits of good nutrition:

» Healthy immune system
» Helps fight and prevent illness
» Improves sports performance
» Healthy muscle and nerve functions
» Delays aging
» Healthy teeth and gums
» Healthy skin, hair, nails
» Increased productivity – concentration, memory
» Better mood
» Maintain a healthy weight
» More confidence, better self-esteem
» More energy
» Better sleep

Consequences of poor nutrition:

» Reduced immunity, increase in illness and infection
» Behavioural changes
» Mood swings – feeling irritable or anxious

» Reduced productivity – lack of concentration, poor memory
» Fatigue, lack of energy
» Poor muscle and nerve functions
» Unhealthy appearance, lack of confidence, low self-esteem
» Food cravings

Conditions resulting from poor nutrition:

Malnutrition: vitamin and mineral deficiencies.

Anaemia: lack of haemoglobin in red blood cells, caused by a deficiency in iron.

Obesity: increased susceptibility to disease (cardiovascular disease, type 2 diabetes, hypertension, high cholesterol and triglycerides).

Carbohydrates (carbs)

Carbohydrates – four calories (4kcal) per gram

45% to 65% of your daily dietary energy (calories)

Carbohydrates are one of the main types of nutrients. They are your body's major source of energy and are stored mainly in your liver and muscles. They help maintain your blood sugar levels, have a protein-sparing role and are a good source of fibre, which helps keep your bowels healthy. When you eat carbs, your body breaks them down into glucose (sugar) and your body then uses it as energy. Glucose is also essential for your brain and muscles (including the heart) to function efficiently.

Too much carbohydrate can result in:

» High triglycerides, weight gain
» High blood sugar levels which could develop into type 2 diabetes
» Becoming insulin resistant

Too little carbohydrate can result in:

» Hypoglycaemia (low blood sugar)
» Lack of energy
» Mild depression
» Constipation
» Poor performance in sport and exercise

There are two major types of carbohydrates in your food – simple and complex.

Simple carbs – also known as simple sugars, are made up of one or two molecules of sugar. They are the quickest source of energy, as they digest rapidly. They are found in refined sugar and lead to fat storage if over consumed. They are:

Monosaccharides (one molecule) – glucose, fructose, galactose

Disaccharides (two molecules) – sucrose, lactose and maltose

Fructose, found in fruit and lactose, found in milk, are natural sugars, not added and are good for you.

Sugars such as high-fructose corn syrup, found in cakes, sweets, biscuits, chocolate, jams, sauces, soups and dressings, are added sugars and are not so good for you!

Complex carbs – also known as starches, are made up of many sugar molecules and are a slower source of energy as they digest more slowly. They are:

Polysaccharides (many molecules) – starch, glycogen and cellulose (fibre). Found in wholegrains, bread, cereals, rice, pasta, potatoes, nuts, seeds, pulses (beans, peas, lentils), fruits and vegetables.

The more complex the carb, the harder it is for your body to break down. Eating brown rice, bread, pasta, etc. is better than eating the white versions. They release energy more slowly and help keep your sugar levels stable.

Fibre

Fibre is a type of carbohydrate found in the indigestible parts of plants. It cannot be broken down by the body and has no calories. There are two types of dietary fibre-soluble and insoluble. Fibre plays a vital role in the smooth running of your body. Some of its functions include:

> » Aids your digestive system, preventing constipation
> » Assists in weight loss/management, curbs appetite, helps you to feel full for longer
> » Helps to delay the absorption of sugar, thus controlling insulin levels and fat storage
> » May help lower the risk of heart disease, diabetes, bad cholesterol and some cancers

Sources of fibre: fruit, vegetables, potatoes, wholegrains,

bran cereals, nuts, seeds, lentils, beans, peas.

Glycaemic index

GI is an excellent way of understanding your good carbs from your bad. It rates the effect carbs have on your blood sugar and insulin levels in your body. The impact they have depends on the type of carb and how quick or slow it is at releasing sugar. Simple carbs are quick releasing, so they have a high glycaemic index. Complex carbs are slower releasing, so they have a lower glycaemic index.

To understand how GI works, each food containing carbohydrates is given a number:

Low GI = 0–55 (ideal)

Med GI = 56–69 (caution)

High GI = 70+ (sparingly, try to avoid)

Benefits of low GI:

- » Promotes a moderate intake of sugars
- » Reduced blood sugar and insulin spikes after food
- » Reduced cravings
- » Reduced appetite
- » Aid weight loss/maintenance

Consequences of high GI:

- » High intake of sugars
- » High blood sugar and insulin spikes followed by lows encouraging overeating
- » Increased hunger and cravings
- » Reduced rate of weight loss

» Weight gain
» Risk of developing type 2 diabetes and cardiovascular disease

Combining foods can reduce the GI of a meal. If you eat a carbohydrate with a protein, it will take longer for the carb to break down, for example, beans on toast, or chicken, potatoes and vegetables. Adding soluble fibre can also have this effect as it slows down the absorption of sugars in carbs.

All carbs provide the same amount of calories per gram, but when it comes to weight loss and good health, the quality of the carb is very important. Good carbs can help control your hunger, sugar intake and weight. They can also decrease the risk of developing some serious health issues.

Proteins

Protein – four calories (4kcal) per gram

10% to 35% of your daily dietary energy (calories)

Protein is needed for growth and repair of body tissues and cells and is found primarily in muscle. It is a secondary source of energy and the most satisfying nutrient as it keeps you feeling full for longer. Proteins are also needed for the production of enzymes, hormone functions (insulin, blood sugar levels), transport functions (haemoglobin, carries oxygen around the body) and immune functions (antibodies, fight infections).

When you eat protein-type foods, your body breaks

them down into amino acids. There are approximately 21 amino acids:

- » Ten are essential, which means your body cannot make them, so you need to get them through your diet
- » Five are non-essential, which means your body can make them
- » Six are conditional essential, which means they are needed for different times of your life, such as certain times of growth or illness

There are two types of protein in food:

Complete proteins *(animal)*

These contain all the essential amino acids that your body needs and primarily come from animal sources such as meat, poultry, fish, eggs and dairy products.

Incomplete proteins *(plant)*

These proteins are missing one or more essential amino acids and they are found in plant-type foods such as grains, nuts, seeds, beans, peas and lentils.

Incomplete proteins can be combined with each other or combined with small amounts of animal sources to make a complete protein, for instance, beans on toast or macaroni and cheese.

Consuming too much protein causes:

- » Increased workload for your kidneys
- » Increased calcium lost in the urine
- » Dehydration

» Bad breath
» Weight gain – some excess protein is excreted and the rest is converted into fat and stored in the body
» It has no additional benefits to health or muscle building

Consuming too little protein causes:

» Muscle wasting
» Poor recovery from a workout
» Fatigue
» Impaired immune function

Fats

Fat – nine calories (9kcal) per gram

20% to 35% of your daily dietary energy (calories)

Fat is a source of energy, protects and cushions your vital organs and insulates your body. It is needed for your hormones, transports vitamins and acts as messengers to let your brain know how full or empty of energy you are (leptin).

There are three main types of fat in your food, saturated fats, trans fats and unsaturated fats (monounsaturated and polyunsaturated).

Saturated fats

Saturated fats are typically solid at room temperature. They increase your bad cholesterol (LDLs). They tend to come from animal sources; meat, dairy products, cream, butter, milk, cheese and some plant forms such as palm or coconut oil.

Trans fats

The majority of trans fats are artificially created and are made during the processing of food. They occur when hydrogen is added to vegetable oil to make it more solid (hydrogenation). They are found in fast foods and where vegetable oil is reheated at high temperatures. They decrease good cholesterol (HDLs) and increase the bad (LDLs), increasing your risk of heart disease and stroke. They are also an appetite stimulant, so the more you eat, the more you want.

Trans fats are found in:

- » Cakes, biscuits
- » Chocolate, sweets
- » Crisps
- » Fast foods, pizza
- » Fried foods, chips
- » Sausage rolls, pies

Unsaturated fats

Monounsaturated and polyunsaturated

Typically liquid at room temperature, they are known as the good fats, as they lower your bad cholesterol (LDLs) and maintain your good (HDLs).

Monounsaturated sources include:

- » Oils – olive, canola, rapeseed, peanut
- » Fruit – Avocados, olives
- » Nuts – hazelnuts, almonds

> » Seeds – pumpkin, sesame

Polyunsaturated sources include:
> » Oily fish – salmon, mackerel, herring, sardines, tuna
> » Oils – sunflower, corn, soybean
> » Seeds – flaxseeds, sunflower
> » Nuts – walnuts, pecan

Polyunsaturated fats are good sources of Omega 3 and 6, which are essential for good health. Your body cannot make them, so you need to get them from your diet. You can also get them in fortified foods.

Triglycerides are a type of fat in your blood and are generated from your diet. When you eat food, your body converts it into energy. When you eat more food than your body needs, the excess is converted into triglycerides and stored in your fat cells (adipose tissue), also known as body fat. If there are too many stored, it will result in weight gain/obesity. There are two main types of body fat, subcutaneous fat and visceral fat.

Subcutaneous fat is found around your body beneath your skin. It is the fat you have most of but it is considered less harmful than visceral fat as it insulates and cushions your body. Too much, though, can put pressure on your heart, breathing and joints.

Visceral fat is found around your middle (abdominal fat) and your vital organs. It is known as central obesity and is linked to an increased risk of heart disease, insulin resistance and type 2 diabetes. Although visceral fat is more dangerous than subcutaneous fat, when you exercise you will lose visceral fat first.

Saturated and unsaturated fat provide the same amount of calories (nine calories per gram), therefore you need to choose wisely for good health. Saturated and trans fats can raise your triglycerides and cholesterol, whereas unsaturated fats can help lower them.

Water

Water has a vital role in your body. It accounts for approximately 60% to 70% of your bodyweight depending on your age, sex, health and weight/muscle. Your body loses water through breathing, digestion and perspiration, so you must rehydrate by drinking fluids and eating foods with high water content.

Functions of water:

- » Protects the body, tissues and organs
- » Hydrates you
- » Regulates body temperature
- » Lubricates joints
- » Helps maintain the balance of bodily fluids
- » Flushes out waste products and toxins
- » Aids digestion
- » Quenches thirst
- » Transports nutrients and oxygen to your cells

Nearly all the major systems in your body depend on water.

Benefits of water:

»   Aids weight loss
»   Helps suppress appetite
»   Can boost your body's ability to burn fat
»   Eases burden on kidneys and liver
»   Helps prevent constipation
»   Prevents dehydration
»   Helps with acne
»   Improves energy levels
»   Helps prevent muscle cramp

How the lack of water affects the body:

»   Dehydration:

   Dehydration occurs when you do not consume enough fluid for your body to function correctly. You will know if you are dehydrated by the colour of your urine as it should be pale yellow. The only time it should be dark yellow is first thing in the morning because of having been asleep.

   If even mildly dehydrated, your metabolism may slow down. It will reduce blood volume, which can reduce the supply of oxygen to your muscles. This process will make you feel tired, both physically and mentally. A lack of fluid can also cause headaches, cramps, decreased performance, weakness and irritability.

»   Fluid Retention:

   One of the main causes of fluid retention is the lack of water in your diet. When your body doesn't get enough water, it retains it for survival. It can show up in the body as swollen feet, legs, hands, face and stomach.

» Fat metabolism:
Your kidneys eliminate waste products with the aid of water. If your body is not getting enough water, your kidneys cannot function properly. As a result, your liver will have to take over some of the kidneys' functions. One of the roles of the liver is to metabolise fat. If the liver is doing some of your kidneys' work, it won't be able to do this efficiently. Therefore when trying to lose weight, the fat-metabolising function of the liver is important.

To avoid dehydration and fluid retention, keep your kidneys functioning properly and put less stress on your liver, it is important to increase your water/fluid intake.

Foods rich with water:

Fruit, vegetables, milk, milkshakes, soup, yoghurt, juices, tea, coffee, herbal tea. Also, food cooked in water, like rice and pasta.

Raise your water intake as it helps with weight loss, your body's ability to burn fat, controlling your appetite and energy. Drinking water before meals could help you to feel less hungry and may result in fewer calories consumed. Aim to drink six to eight glasses per day, but this may vary depending on what food you eat (water-rich foods), how physically active you are, the climate you live in and illness.

Alcohol

Provides seven calories per gram

Alcohol is the only other substance that provides energy (calories) but is not classed as a macronutrient. It isn't essential for life and causes stress on your body. It's a depressant and can affect your thoughts, feelings and behaviour.

You may find having a few alcoholic beverages can make you feel more relaxed. This is due to chemical changes that occur in your brain in response to the alcohol. It can depress the part associated with inhibition (self-consciousness, shyness, wariness) therefore you feel more confident and less reserved. If you continue to drink more, other parts of your brain start to be affected, increasing the probability of adverse emotional reactions. You may become more aggressive, angry, argumentative and depressed.

When it comes to your food choices, drinking too much alcohol can decrease your self-control. Because of this, you could end up eating more food containing high fat and sugar. As alcohol lowers your blood sugars, you will probably crave these foods the next day and all good intentions go out the window.

Severe alcohol consumption interferes with the central nervous system's (brain and spinal cord) ability to send, receive and understand information from all parts of your body. Your body treats it as a toxin and it can only process one unit of alcohol per hour. Depending on your ability to process and clear the alcohol from your body, you could be facing some serious illnesses.

Alcohol is linked to:

- » Depression, anxiety, stress
- » Suicide, psychosis
- » Memory loss
- » Altering brain chemistry
- » Low energy levels
- » Weight gain – alcohol is metabolised to fat
- » Cravings
- » Sleep disturbances
- » Hypertension (high blood pressure)
- » Dehydration
- » Muscle cramps
- » Reduced fertility
- » Type 2 diabetes
- » Liver damage
- » Reduced kidney function
- » Some cancers
- » Road traffic accidents

Recommended limits on alcohol units vary in different countries. For example, in Ireland, it is 17 units per week for men and 11 for women. In England, it is 14 units for both men and women. It is also advised to have two to three alcohol-free days per week.

The number of units in an alcoholic drink is based on the size of the drink and its alcohol strength.

Calculating units: strength (ABV) x volume (ML) divided by 1,000

Pint of lager

4.3% ABV (strength)
568ml (volume)
4.3 x 568 divided by 1,000
= 2.44 units

Bottle of red wine

14% ABV (strength)
750ml (volume)
14 X 750 divided by 1,000
= 10.5 units

Binge drinking is consuming more than six standard drinks in one session. Done regularly, it can be harmful to your health.

New Habit: reduce alcohol

- » Stick to units allowed
- » Alternate each drink with a glass of water
- » Drink slowly, pace yourself
- » Mix wine with soda or sparkling water or put a couple of ice cubes in it
- » Drink glasses rather than pints
- » Don't drink on an empty stomach
- » Don't get into rounds when out socialising

Alcohol provides no nutritional value but plenty of calories. It cannot be stored in the body and suppresses the metabolism of carbs and fats and the fat-burning process. It lowers your blood sugar, increasing your cravings for high-fat, high-sugar foods. Therefore it would be advisable to exclude alcohol or at least reduce your alcohol consumption when trying to lose weight and for better health.

Caffeine

The world's most popular stimulant, it perks you up and releases adrenaline. Caffeine can alleviate fatigue, increase energy levels and aid concentration. On the other hand, too much caffeine can cause insomnia, nervousness, irritability, fast heartbeat and muscle tremors.

Check the volume of caffeine you are consuming in a day, such as coffee, tea, Coke and energy drinks. Be mindful of energy drinks, as they are high in sugar and can have an effect on your blood pressure and heart rhythm. Limit lattes and cappuccinos as they can contain a lot of calories.

Safe consumption per day:

- » Adults: up to 400mg
- » Pregnant women: less than 200mg
- » Children: less than 100mg

Sugar

Sugar can be detrimental to your health and cause a lot of distress for people, affecting their diet and influencing their behaviour. Consuming too much sugar can lead to weight gain/obesity, type 2 diabetes and heart disease. It can also lead to tooth decay, reduced energy, poor concentration, mood swings, food cravings and addiction. (Sugar can have the same effect as an addictive drug.)

We know cakes, biscuits, sweets, chocolate and fizzy drinks contain sugar, but there are other foods that you may not think about, including:

- » Flavoured waters
- » Juice
- » Salami, pepperoni and other dried meats
- » Energy bars and drinks
- » Breakfast cereals – some can have a lot of sugar
- » Fruit yoghurts
- » Salad dressings
- » Tomato ketchup
- » Tinned soups
- » Pasta sauces
- » Gravy granules
- » Peanuts – honey roasted, seasoned, dry roasted
- » Burger buns, bagels
- » Crackers
- » Low-fat dishes
- » Processed foods

There are many names for sugar, such as glucose, fructose, lactose, sucrose, maltose, dextrose, high-fructose corn syrup, molasses, treacle and honey, to name a few.

Look at food labels on a product. If you are aware of the amount of sugar in products, you can make better choices when considering which foods to eat and drink. Limit your intake of sugar to 6tsp/25g per day (4g = 1tsp).

Fad diets

Characteristics of fad diets:

- » Weight loss is rapid, which can slow down your metabolism
- » Numerous marketing claims made
- » By their nature offer only a quick fix
- » Restrictive; elimination of one or more food groups

Fad diets are hard to adhere to long term and you will probably end up putting all your weight back on and even more. They are linked to eating disorders, encourage yo-yo dieting and can be nutritionally deficient as they are restrictive. They also promote cravings and feelings of guilt if you cannot stick to them.

Do not exclude any food group from your diet as you need all groups for different reasons to maintain good health. It's all about what type of food you eat from each food group and the quantity.

Fast food

Why do so many choose fast food?

- » Pleasurable in taste
- » Busy lifestyles
- » Lack of time to cook
- » Fussy eaters
- » Low cost
- » Less hassle

» Prepared quickly
» Smart marketing presented in an attractive way

Fast food is not good for your health. It has low nutritional value and is high in calories, sugar, fat, salt and additives. I'm not saying you can never have fast food. Nevertheless, if you consume it too frequently, it will increase your risk of weight gain, cardiovascular disease and type 2 diabetes.

Shopping

Your shopping list is important when it comes to food choices and successful change. You need to have a look at what types of food you are regularly buying. How healthy/unhealthy are they? See how you can improve your shopping choices over the next few weeks. Which items do you think you can remove and what could you buy more of instead?

Tips for successful shopping:

» Always know what you want.
» Make a list and stick to it.
» Don't shop hungry.
» Ignore advertisements unless they are beneficial to you.
» Beware of bulk buying. Don't need it, don't buy it.
» Avoid special offers unless you need them.
» Know the layout of the store and avoid the aisles you have difficulty saying no to.
» Your food choices can often be made

unconsciously, so pay attention and be mindful when shopping.

Eating out

Whether in a restaurant or someone else's house, eating out is a great way to socialise with family or friends. Just because you are trying to lose weight doesn't mean you can't eat out occasionally. Eating out doesn't mean you have to eat poorly or overindulge. There are many things you can do to help you when dining out. It's changing your attitude and your approach to eating out that is key.

- » Check the menu before you go
- » No bread at the table
- » Share a starter
- » Share a dessert
- » If having a starter skip the dessert or vice versa
- » For the main course, choose chicken, fish, or lean meat with veg
- » Swap chips for salad or boiled or baked potatoes
- » Avoid battered fish, chicken, etc.
- » Avoid creamy soups or sauces
- » Ask for dressings on the side
- » Choose grilled, boiled, or stir-fry
- » Watch alcohol intake over the meal, also drink some water
- » Coffee – choose Americano rather than latte or cappuccino

If eating salads, be mindful of what they contain. Be

careful of dressings, croutons, potato salad, coleslaw, cheese, etc. Flavour your salad with balsamic vinegar and a little extra-virgin olive oil, lemon or lime juice, or low-calorie salad dressing (check sugar content).

Home cooking

Pick out a few recipes and familiarise yourself on how to cook them. When you cook at home, you have more control over what you are eating. It encourages family time and a healthier attitude towards food.

Flavours to add to your food are herbs, spices, garlic, curry powder or paste, lemon or lime juice, salt (pinch), pepper, etc.

Healthy cooking methods are baking, grilling, boiling, poaching, steaming, stir-frying and roasting (use low-calorie spray).

Nutritional guidelines:

- » Find a balance between food intake and physical activity
- » Stay within your calorie needs
- » Make smart choices from every food group – choose nutritional foods
- » Eat a variety of fruit and vegetables
- » Eat more fish (Omega 3)
- » Drink more water and eat more water-based foods
- » Reduce sugar and salt intake
- » Cook more homemade food
- » Choose healthy snacks
- » Reduce alcohol

» Eat less processed and fast foods
» Reduce fizzy drinks

Good nutrition = Macronutrients and micronutrients
Essential amino acids
Omega 3 and 6
Water
Fibre

What you eat today dictates how you feel tomorrow. If your food intake comes from poor nutrition, you will feel tired, irritable and moody. On the other hand, if your intake of food comes from good nutrition, you will feel better, more energised and happier. Even though a calorie is a calorie, the quality of your calories is essential for your body to function properly.

EAT WELL TO STAY WELL

CHAPTER SEVENTEEN

Vitamins

Below is a brief description of what role each vitamin has in your body and some examples of what foods contain them.

Water-soluble vitamins

Vitamin C

An antioxidant, protecting all cells. Assists in the absorption of iron and a healthy immune system. Forms collagen that helps maintain healthy body tissue, e.g. the skin. Aids wound healing.

   Sources: fruit, especially citrus, tomatoes, apples, berries, peppers, green veg, potatoes.

Vitamin B1: Thiamine

Energy metabolism (converts food into energy). Promotes growth, normal muscle function, healthy nervous system.

   Sources: red meat, wholegrains, nuts, seeds, beans, peas, fortified foods.

Vitamin B2: Riboflavin

Energy metabolism. Normal growth and cell function, healthy skin and eyes.

Sources: dairy products, green veg, eggs, red meat, liver, fish, nuts, fortified food.

Vitamin B3: Niacin

Energy metabolism. A healthy nervous system, digestion and skin.

Sources: fish, poultry, red meat, nuts, wholegrains, fortified foods.

Vitamin B5: Pantothenic acid

Energy metabolism, aids red blood cells and hormone production.

Sources: poultry, red meat, fish, eggs, mushrooms, avocados, wholegrains, seeds.

Vitamin B6: Pyridoxine

Energy metabolism. Aids formation of red blood cells, healthy nervous and immune systems and skin.

Sources: red meat, liver, poultry, fish, beans, peas, nuts, seeds, bananas, avocados, potatoes, green veg, fortified foods.

Vitamin B7: Biotin

Energy metabolism. Healthy nervous system, skin, hair and nails.

Sources: liver, red meat, nuts, seeds, fish, eggs.

Vitamin B9: Folic acid, folate

Healthy cells, nervous and immune systems. Prevents birth defects, helps with forming red blood cells, energy metabolism.

Sources: green veg, fruit, avocados, liver, eggs, nuts, seeds, beans, peas, wholegrains, fortified foods.

Vitamin B12: Cobalamin

Production of red blood cells, healthy nervous and immune systems, promotes growth, energy metabolism.

Sources: red meat, liver, poultry, fish, dairy products, eggs, fortified foods.

Fat-soluble vitamins

Vitamin A: Retinol

An antioxidant. Healthy vision, growth and development, healthy bones, immune system and skin.

Sources: liver, dairy products, eggs, fish, fortified foods. Foods containing beta carotene, e.g. carrots, green veg, peppers, tomatoes, oranges and other naturally colourful foods. Beta carotene converts to vitamin A in the body.

Vitamin D

Aids in the absorption of calcium and phosphorus in the body. A healthy immune system, bones, teeth and muscles.

Sources: the primary source is sunlight absorption

on bare skin. Also found in oily fish, eggs, dairy products, fortified foods.

Vitamin E

An antioxidant, protecting your cells, healthy immune system and skin.

Sources: vegetable oils, nuts, seeds, wheat germ, eggs, green veg, fruit, avocados, fortified foods.

Vitamin K

Needed for normal blood clotting, healthy bones. Made by gut bacteria.

Sources: green veg, eggs, fruit, avocados, veg oils.

CHAPTER EIGHTEEN

Minerals

Below are brief descriptions of what role each mineral has in your body and some examples of what foods contain them.

Calcium:

Formation and maintenance of healthy bones and teeth, normal nerve and muscle functions, assists in blood clotting.

    Sources: dairy products, tinned fish, green veg, nuts, seeds, beans, peas, lentils, tofu, fortified foods.

Magnesium

Energy metabolism, helps regulate insulin, healthy bones, teeth and nervous system, normal muscle function, protein synthesis.

    Sources: wholegrains, seeds, nuts, beans, peas, green veg, fruit, avocados, bananas, fish.

Potassium

Regulates fluid balance, healthy nervous system, normal muscle functions, energy metabolism, aids blood pressure.

Sources: green veg, potatoes, fruit, bananas, oranges, red meat, beans, peas, nuts, seeds, dairy products, fish.

Phosphorus

Formation of teeth and bones, the growth and repair of cells and tissues. Energy metabolism.

Sources: fish, red meat, poultry, dairy products, eggs, seeds, nuts, beans, peas, wholegrains.

Sodium

Maintains fluid balance in the body, normal nerve and muscle functions.

Sources: table salt, processed foods, meat products, sauces, soups, smoked foods.

Sulphur

Protects cells, protein synthesis and healthy skin.

Sources: fish, poultry, red meat, eggs, dairy products, nuts, green veg.

Chloride

Aids fluid and acid balance in the body, aids digestion.

Sources: table salt, vegetables, seaweed, tomatoes.

Iron

Important for many cell functions, the production of haemoglobin in red blood cells, helps prevent anaemia, aids energy metabolism.

Sources: liver, red meat, poultry, fish, nuts, seeds, eggs, green veg, peas, beans, lentils, wholegrains, fortified foods.

Chromium

Regulates insulin, energy metabolism.

Sources: green veg, potatoes, wholegrains, poultry, red meat.

Zinc

Growth and development, healthy immune system, aids wound healing, energy metabolism, proper taste and smell, healthy skin and eyes.

Sources: red meat, poultry, fish, dairy products, eggs, beans, peas, lentils, seeds, nuts, wholegrains.

Manganese

Protects cells, bone development, energy metabolism, regulates blood sugar.

Sources: nuts, green veg, wholegrains, beans, peas, lentils, fruit, pineapple.

Copper

Assists production of red blood cells, healthy bones and immune system.

Sources: liver, fish, nuts, seeds, wholegrains.

Selenium

An antioxidant, protects cells, thyroid health and a healthy immune system.

Sources: nuts, seeds, fish, red meat, poultry, wholegrains, eggs, dairy products.

Fluoride

Healthy teeth. Fights tooth decay.
  Sources: tap water, fortified systems, dental products, fish.

Iodine

Produces thyroid hormones, regulates metabolism.
  Sources: seafood, iodized salt, dairy products.

CHAPTER NINETEEN

Food Diary

A food diary is very beneficial for self-monitoring. It helps you to become aware of the food you eat and drink. It enables you to track your food intake and highlights your eating habits. It helps you to evaluate your diet, identifying problem areas and where improvements can be made.

Analysing your diary:

- » Look at your food consumption over the week – how healthy is it?
- » How much fruit and how many vegetables did you eat?
- » Wholegrain-to-white ratio
- » The amount of sugar and salt – check labels
- » What was your fluid intake, good or bad? Some drinks can be loaded with sugar and calories
- » How big were your portion sizes?
- » Your food preparation – how much was home-cooked?
- » Your times of eating
- » Where did you eat – at the kitchen table, watching TV, on the go?

» How you felt

When evaluating your diary, ask yourself:

» Is your diet balanced? Think about the food pyramid
» What changes can you make over the next week?
» Where can calories be cut or eliminated?
» What unhealthy foods are you eating too frequently?
» Could there be a reason for this?
» If you snack, does it trigger further eating?

Some people can handle having snacks and some can't. If you're a person that eats until full or is susceptible to overindulging, then you may need to stick to just having three meals a day and no snacking. Perhaps you need more structure to your diet, so you may need to do some meal planning.

Your food diary can also identify emotional eating. When you look back over your diary, what emotional triggers are evident? Were you stressed or anxious? Were you bored? If you overindulged, how did it make you feel? Where did you eat? Was it a particular time of the day? Sometimes, where you ate and what time of the day it was can provide insight into emotional triggers for your eating habits.

Food diary tips

It's good practice not to wait until the end of the day to

record what you have consumed throughout the day. Try to write it down as soon as you can after eating. This way, it will help eliminate the possibility of you leaving anything out.

You need to include all the extras – the ones you don't think really count. Butter on the potatoes, mayo on your sandwich, the piece of cheese you ate while looking in the fridge, the bit you took from someone else's plate, or the few crisps you took when opening your child's bag. You may be shocked at just how much you nibble and the fact that all these extras add up.

Don't exclude the days when you overindulge. When these days occur, maybe you decide not to keep a record because you feel guilty that you have slipped up or you're embarrassed about your eating habits. You think it wouldn't look good written down in black and white. These are very significant days to record, as you can get a great insight into your food habits.

Use whatever kind of food diary works for you. Create your own system – whatever keeps you recording without putting you under pressure. Most importantly, be honest, you're only fooling yourself if you're not. Think of how invaluable a food diary can be.

Example of a food diary 1

Day/Date/ Time	Food	Drink	Where you ate How you Feel
Monday 15/02/2016 10:00 am	2 Weetabix with skimmed milk 1 banana glass of water	Cup of coffee with milk	Ate at kitchen table Feel good and ready for my walk
12:00pm	2 choc biscuits	Mug of coffee with milk	Ate at my desk Feel guilty for eating the biscuits

Example of a food diary 2

Date/time	Meal	Food	Qty.	Drink	Where you ate
15/02/2016 09:00am	Breakfast	Weetabix, skimmed milk	2	Cup of tea with skimmed milk	Ate in sitting room watching breakfast TV
Record feelings at the end of the day:					

CHAPTER TWENTY

Food Labelling

Food labelling provides you with information about the product you are purchasing. Under strict regulation, suppliers are required to provide complete information on the product:

1. Ingredients, including allergens (listed in descending order by weight)
2. Quantity/weight
3. Name of food
4. Storage instructions
5. Use by date/best before date
6. Clear preparation and cooking instructions
7. Name and address of manufacturer
8. Batch number
9. Place of origin
10. Any genetically modified ingredients
11. Beverages which contain >1.2% alcohol

Ingredients list: this is in descending order. It shows what the product contains, including additives. (The first ingredient is what the product contains most of.) They must also show allergens, e.g. nuts, fish, eggs, milk, gluten, etc.

Use by date: product not to be eaten after this date.

Best before date: product can be eaten after this date. It's more about the quality of the product. It may lose flavour or texture after this date.

Other information found on labels

Nutritional information:

Energy – kj/kcal per 100g/100ml
Fat and saturated fat (g)
Carbohydrates and sugars (g)
Protein (g)
Salt (g)
Fibre (g)
Reference intakes
Vitamins and minerals added to the product

Shopping guidelines

Traffic lights system	Red	Amber	Green
Per 100g	High	Medium	Low
Fat	>17.5g	3–17.5g	<3g
Saturated Fat	>5g	1.5–5g	<1.5g
Sugar (4g = 1 tsp)	>22.5g	5–22.5g	<5g
Salt (6g = 1 tsp)	>1.5g	0.3–1.5g	<0.3g

What the claims on a product mean:

Low fat: solids – <3g fat per 100g; liquids – <1.5g per 100ml

95 percent fat free: The product contains 5 percent fat, or 5g per 100g

Fat free: <0.5g fat per 100g/100ml

Low in saturates: solids – <1.5g per 100g; liquids – <0.75g per 100ml

Reduced fat: 30 percent less fat than the standard product

Low sugar: <5g sugar per 100g; <2.5g per 100ml

Sugar free: <0.5g sugar per 100g/100ml

No added sugar: no sugars (monosaccharides or disaccharides) have been added, but the product may have other carbs or natural sugars present (naturally occurring sugars should appear on label)

Low salt: <0.3g of salt per 100g (low sodium – <0.12g per 100g)

Very low salt: 0.1g of salt per 100g (very low sodium – <0.04g per 100g) (2.5g of salt = 1g of sodium)

High fibre: 6g per 100g; 3g per 100kcal

Source of fibre: 3g per 100g; 1.5g per 100kcal

Low calorie solids: <40kcal per 100g

Low calorie liquids: <20kcal per 100ml

Calorie free: <4kcal per 100ml

Reduced calorie: 30 percent fewer calories than the

standard product (depending on how many calories are in the product, it still could contain a lot of calories).

If a product claims to be low fat, check that it doesn't contain large amounts of added sugar and salt to replace the flavour of fat.

If a product says it has, for example, 8g of sugar, divide it by four (4g to 1tsp) to see how many teaspoons of sugar it contains (8/4 = 2 tsp).

Carbohydrates and Protein (4kcal per gram): multiply the grams of carbs or proteins by 4 to give you how many calories the product contains for each one.

Fats (9kcal per gram): multiply the grams of fat by 9 to give you how many calories the product contains of fat. Do the same to see how much is unsaturated.

If a product's ingredients list contains hydrogenated oil, it contains trans fats.

It would be good practice to learn how to read labels on products. Check the labels, especially for sugar, salt, saturated and trans fats.

Food additives are any substances added to food that serve a purpose. For instance, to maintain or improve the nutritional composition, freshness, safety, texture, appearance, taste, etc. Some examples of these are colourings, emulsifiers, stabilisers, flavour enhancers, sweeteners, preservatives and antioxidants. In Europe, they appear on labels as E numbers, making it easier to identify what has been added to a product. The

European Food Safety Authority must also approve them before they can get an E number.

Examples of E numbers:

E100s – colours, e.g. E102 tartrazine, a yellow colour for drinks and confectionery.

E200s – preservatives, e.g. E210 benzoic acid, a preservative in beer.

E300s – antioxidants, e.g. E321 BHT (butylated hydroxytoluene), helps prevents fat going rancid.

E400s – emulsifiers/stabilisers/thickeners, e.g. E415 xanthan gum, a stabiliser and thickener used in salad dressings.

E600s – flavour enhancers, e.g. E621 monosodium glutamate, adds flavour to food.

E900s – sweeteners, e.g. E951 aspartame, a sugar substitute in food.

Food colouring is a dye, pigment, or other substance added to a food or beverage to enhance or add colour. It's used to replace colour lost due to exposure to light, air moisture and other conditions. It provides colour to colourless foods and corrects natural variation in colour.

Preservatives are added to prolong shelf life, keep food fresh and to fight bacteria, mould, etc.

Antioxidants slow down the rate of oxidation of foods (substance exposed to oxygen in the air) and extend shelf life. Some are natural and some are artificially created, e.g. a cut apple exposed to the air goes brown. Fats such as butter start to smell if left out of the fridge.

Emulsifiers enable oil and water to mix, e.g. in mayonnaise. They maintain the structure and texture of food, which makes food more appealing.

Stabilisers smoothen and give a firmer texture to food. They assist emulsifiers.

Flavour enhancers are used to improve or intensify flavours, e.g. monosodium glutamate (MSG), which is present in many processed foods.

Sweeteners are added to food to provide sweetness to replace or reduce sugar and decrease calories, e.g. aspartame, saccharin, sucralose, sorbitol, stevia, etc.

Food additives get a bad press, but not all additives are bad for you. You may like to investigate and find out more information.

CHAPTER TWENTY-ONE
Healthy, Happy, Life

Your new approach to obtain a healthier, happier and more fulfilling life.

Take responsibility

» Accept that it's up to you to take charge of your life and nobody else.
» When something happens to upset you, it's your ability to cope with it that determines the outcome.
» Remember, no one is immune to pain. It's how you deal with it.
» Live life consciously and be aware of what's going on around you, knowing what you're doing and accepting responsibility for it.

Stop the excuses and the blame game

» Stop making excuses and blaming others.
» Accept other people's personalities. Accept them for who they are, not who you want them to be.
» Listen to other perspectives or opinions. You

might learn something.
- » Be open-minded. You don't have to agree.
- » Listening is a powerful tool.

Challenge your belief system and change your limiting beliefs

- » If what you are doing isn't working for you, change it.
- » You need to acknowledge it to change it.
- » You need to believe to succeed or achieve.
- » Get out of your comfort zone.

Stress management and quality sleep

- » Learn how to manage your stress.
- » Meditate, use mindfulness, deep breathing exercises, have a massage, etc.
- » Do whatever it takes.
- » Try to get seven or eight hours of sleep per night.
- » Go to bed early as often as you can.
- » Leave mobile phones and laptops outside the bedroom.

Become aware and take notice of your behaviours and habits

- » Do they move you closer to achieving what you want or further away?
- » What behaviours and habits can you install over time that will assist you in achieving your goals?

» Put the cues in place to trigger yourself to do something. I think these are essential when it comes to installing new habits (notes on the fridge door, in a calendar, items put around the house).
» Remember, the life changes you make are changes for the better!

Set a SMART goal

» What do you want? The emotional reasoning.
» Give yourself a clear picture of what you want.
» Visualise what you want. The more you visualise and tell yourself something, the better chance you have of achieving it.
» What do you have to do, what are you willing to do?
» Are your goals in line with your values?
» If you want something, take action.

How can you improve your nutrition?

» Come up with ways to change unhealthy habits.
» What foods do you like?
» What are you willing to eat?
» How much fruit and how many vegetables, what kinds?
» What foods are you willing to reduce or give up?
» Increase your fluid intake

Exercise – move more

- » When it comes to exercise, do something you enjoy.
- » Don't overstress yourself, especially at the beginning, or you won't keep doing it.
- » When you get fitter, you can progress to more challenging exercises.
- » You don't need to exercise for long periods.
- » If you are not getting the results you want, reassess. Maybe get some advice.
- » Even if you do not have much time, don't say "why bother?" – it's better to do something than nothing at all.

Keep focused, remain consistent and persevere

- » Find the motivation.
- » Keep a diary.
- » Get support from family and friends.
- » It's normal to meet resistance, but that doesn't mean it's not going to work. It's part of the challenge. Keep focused on what you are trying to accomplish and you will get there in the end.

Be your own best friend

- » You let people know how to treat you by the way you treat yourself.
- » Mistakes are learning purposes.
- » Watch your "self-talk". It's crucial when it comes

to your health and wellbeing.

» Make positive affirmations. Positive thinking gives you more power to succeed and helps you handle whatever life throws at you.
» You do not have to be perfect.
» Your best is good enough.
» The past has no hold on you unless you let it.
» The power is within you.

It doesn't matter how much knowledge you gain if you do not use it. It will take time and effort, but the reward is huge.

At the end of the day, you only have one life. You only get one shot at it. There's no dress rehearsal. Life will have its challenges and you will probably run into some difficult times and painful events. But if you keep thinking you won't cope, or that you will always fail, then you won't try anything new and you will stay the way you are. You have to challenge yourself and try new things. It's never too late to change.

LET MAKING YOURSELF HAPPY BE THE BEST JOB YOU'VE EVER HAD.

Sleep + Nutrition + Exercise

Beliefs + Emotions + Behaviours

Habits + Values + Goals

Actions + Positivity + Responsibility

- Stress - Fears - Negativity

= Health + Happiness + Wellbeing

COURSES **AND**
Qualifications

Mindstream Success Coaching and Training Ltd.

Diploma in Life and Business Coaching

Litton Lane Training

Exercise and Fitness Instruction and Personal Training

Shaw's Academy

Health and Fitness and Personal Nutrition

Many thanks to the above organisations for allowing me to use some of the information I learned through their courses in order for me to compile this book.

Health and wellbeing are so complex, and there's a lot of information out there for you to investigate. I just wanted to get you to think about your health, not just diet and exercise, but also other areas that can enhance your life.

Index

A

Actions 88
Acts of kindness 43
Aerobic 112
Aerobic exercises 120
Affirmations 93
Alcohol 138
Anaemia 126
Anaerobic 113
Anaerobic exercises 121

B

Basal metabolic rate 111
Behaviours 74
Belief system 28
Blood pressure 21
Breaking through the barriers 79

C

Caffeine 141
Carbohydrates 126
Cardiovascular disease 17
Cardiovascular training 115
Cholesterol 20
Circuit training 119
Cognitive behavioural therapy 82
Complete proteins 131
Complex carbs, 128
Cortisol 58

D

Delayed gratification 95
Diabetes 18

E

Eating out 145
Emotions 41, 45
E numbers 165
Exercise 67, 107

F

Fad diets 143
Fast food 143
Fats 132
Fear 41, 51, 94
Fibre 128
Flexibility 122
Food addiction 14
Food additives 164
Food diary 156
Food diary examples 159, 160
Food labelling 161

G

Get to grips with your emotions 49
Glycaemic index 129
Goals 100
Goal setting 42, 101
Gratitude 41

H

Habits 84
Happiness 37
Home cooking 146
Hormones 55
Hypertension 22

I

Incomplete proteins 131
Insulin 55

L

Leptin 57

M

Macro-nutrients 124
Meditation 66
Metabolic rate 111
Metabolism 111
Micro-nutrients 124
Mindfulness 66
Minerals 125, 152
Monounsaturated 133
Motivation 80, 94

N

Natural and unnatural emotions
        47
Nutrition 124
Nutritional guidelines 146
Nutritional information 162

O

Obesity 11

P

Polyunsaturated 133
Powerful beliefs 32
Proteins 130

R

Relapses 77, 82
Resistance exercises 121

Resistance training 116
Responsibility 90

S

Saturated fats 132
Self esteem 38
Self-talk 91
Shopping 144
Shopping guidelines 162
Simple carbs 127
Sleep 60
Stages of change 74
States of mind 53
Stress 63
Stress management 66
Subcutaneous fat 134
Sugar 141
Sugar addiction 16

T

Training zones 112
Trans fats 133
Triglycerides 134
Types of training 115

U

Unsaturated fats 133

V

Values 70
Visceral fat 134
Visualisation 96
Vitamins 125, 148

W

Water 135